Combative Politics

Combative Politics

The Media and Public Perceptions of Lawmaking

MARY LAYTON ATKINSON

THE UNIVERSITY OF CHICAGO PRESS   CHICAGO AND LONDON

The University of Chicago Press, Ltd., London
© 2017 by The University of Chicago
All rights reserved. Published 2017
Printed in the United States of America

26 25 24 23 22 21 20 19 18 17   1 2 3 4 5

ISBN-13: 978-0-226-44189-4 (cloth)
ISBN-13: 978-0-226-44192-4 (paper)
ISBN-13: 978-0-226-44208-2 (e-book)
DOI: 10.7208/chicago/9780226442082.001.0001

Library of Congress Cataloging-in-Publication Data

Names: Atkinson, Mary Layton, author.
Title: Combative politics : the media and public perceptions of lawmaking / Mary Layton
    Atkinson.
Description: Chicago ; London : The University of Chicago Press, 2017. | Includes
    bibliographical references and index.
Identifiers: LCCN 2016037670 | ISBN 9780226441894 (cloth : alk. paper) |
    ISBN 9780226441924 (pbk. : alk. paper) | ISBN 9780226442082 (e-book)
Subjects: LCSH: Mass media—Political aspects—United States. | Political parties—Press
    coverage—United States.
Classification: LCC P95.82.U6 A86 2017 | DDC 302.23/0973—dc23 LC record available at
    https://lccn.loc.gov/2016037670

♾ This paper meets the requirements of ANSI/NISO Z39.48-1992 (Permanence of Paper).

FOR TIM

Contents

Acknowledgments

This book has been many, many years in the making. I have been incredibly fortunate to have the encouragement and guidance of several mentors, colleagues, and family members along the way, without which this project would not have come to fruition. Several programs of the Political Science Department at UNC–Chapel Hill, including the American Politics Research Group (APRG), the George Rabinowitz Seminar, and the Thomas M. Uhlman Graduate Fund, also supported my work. APRG and the Uhlman Fund provided summer research stipends and travel awards that helped to support this research. The George Rabinowitz Seminar graciously provided numerous opportunities to present early drafts of the dissertation chapters. The seminar's participants—and its namesake in particular—offered feedback that has dramatically improved the quality of the project.

I have had the pleasure of working with several research assistants who dedicated hours and hours of their lives to coding the *New York Times* data described here. I appreciate the hard work and dedication to the project offered by Anna Dietrich, Lindsay Tello, Linden Wait, and Jazmine Walker. Additional research assistance was provided by graduate assistants Jenny Kaemmerlen, Tracy Martin Nash, and Tonderai Mushipe. I am thankful to each of them for their attention to detail and their can-do attitudes.

I owe a huge debt of gratitude to my sister, Katharine Atkinson Quince, who painstakingly copyedited the manuscript before it went out for review. Only a sister would do such a thing out of the goodness of her heart. I truly appreciate her time, love, and use of the Oxford comma.

I am so grateful for the feedback provided by Amber Boydstun, Justin Gross, Daniele Kreiss, Mike MacKuen, Jason Roberts, Brian Schaffner,

Jim Stimson, and two anonymous reviewers who read and commented on drafts of the manuscript. Their insights improved the work immeasurably. I also owe special thanks to the members of the Political Science Department at UNC–Charlotte, especially Martha Kropf, Cherie Maestas, John Szmer, Jim Walsh, and Greg Weeks. They were a tremendous source of advice and support. Cherie also generously read chapter drafts and helped me develop the book proposal. I could not ask for better colleagues and know that the revision process would have been much slower and much more painful without them.

I wish to extend wholehearted thanks to Frank Baumgartner for the *many* contributions he has made to the success of this project. To say that he has been generous with his time and resources would be a gross understatement. In fact, I've been known to affectionately refer him as "Obi-Wan" when he's not around because of everything he's done to train me in the ways of the academic force. (I guess the secret is out now.) Over the years, Frank has read countless drafts of chapters—always offering thorough, insightful, and remarkably fast feedback—and read the manuscript in its entirety before it went out for review. Moreover, he has never failed to provide advice, support, and tough love when I've needed it. In his own words, I have in Frank a "mentor for life"—something few people can say and something for which I am truly grateful.

I also owe special thanks to my cheering squad—my amazing family members who have supported me in this endeavor from start to finish. My fantastic in-laws, Sue Wood, Greg Paulson, and Jane Pugliese, have encouraged me with the same love and enthusiasm that they show their children. My parents, Linda and Jim Strong, and Jerry and Robin Atkinson, have always believed I could accomplish anything I put my mind to. They have celebrated all the small victories along the way to the publication of this book, from conference papers given, to chapters completed, and on and on. Their unwavering belief that the project would be a success helped me will this book into existence. I am so grateful for their love and support.

Finally, this book is dedicated to my amazing husband, Tim Paulson. Tim has been there from beginning to end, doing anything and everything humanly possible to help me along on this journey. He has uprooted himself twice in the past eight years for the sake of my career. Both times, he viewed the moves as an adventure and remained positive—even while commuting *four hours a day* to his old job after our move to Charlotte. He has been my sounding board, my editor, my graphic designer, my tech support, and, most of all, he has been an endless well of optimism and encouragement that I have drawn on innumerable times. Simply put, this book is as much Tim's as it is mine. It would not have been possible without him. Thank you Timmy, for everything!

Tables

Figures

Introduction

Conflict Breeds Opposition

Those who believe that Americans don't notice or don't care about how things get done are deluding themselves. . . . Democracy, in other words, is as much about process—how we go about resolving our differences and crafting policy—as it is about result. —Lee Hamilton, former member of the U.S. House of Representatives

Health care reform topped President Clinton's domestic agenda in 1993 and 1994. It also topped the public's agenda. Ninety percent of Americans believed there was a crisis in the nation's health care system (Blenndon et al. 1995) and 74% wanted to see a system of universal coverage put in place (ABC News Poll 1994). The Clinton Administration devised a plan to do just that—one that included a range of provisions supported by huge majorities of the public. But, despite the overwhelming popularity of the policy's individual provisions, the plan itself received lukewarm public support and grew increasingly unpopular over the course of a protracted, partisan debate.

This disconnect between public support for the specifics of a policy and opposition to the plan as a whole has been observed time and again in modern American politics. For instance, public support for President Obama's health reform plan closely paralleled support for the Clinton plan. Many of the policy's specific provisions, like the requirement that insurance companies offer coverage to everyone who applies, were favored by as much as 80% of the public (Kaiser 2009). But the plan itself was far less popular. Opposition to it mounted over the course of a fierce debate in Washington and support for it fell to roughly 40% by the end of 2010.

Many Republican proposals have faced the same fate. Support for the specific substantive provisions of President G. W. Bush's Social Security reforms, the No Child Left Behind Act, and the Federal Marriage Amendment were all much more popular than were the reform packages as a whole.

In this book, I offer a unifying theory that explains why members of the public frequently reject policies that seem to give them exactly what they want. Throughout, I develop and test my theory, which centers on public response to media coverage of the policy-making process—reactions that are distinct from partisan attitudes about specific policies. I demonstrate that the passage of bills with popular provisions can result in a public backlash stemming from exposure (via the news media) to the unpopular process of policy making.

How the Public Sees Policy Making: An Overview

Most people expect the government to help correct the problem of the moment, whether it be the high cost of health care, the ballooning budget deficit, or the insolvency of Social Security. With broad support for reform, lawmakers begin to debate a course of action. With bipartisan support, a reform might become law quickly. But more often, the initial bipartisan agreement that something must be done is eroded by a partisan dispute over what exactly will be done. The negotiations between and within the parties span weeks, months, and sometimes years. All the while the rhetoric becomes more heated and partisan as the stakes increase in proportion to the political capital expended.

Public affairs journalists and editors have incentives to focus on the partisan conflict and debate inherent in the legislative process. Doing so increases the entertainment value of their reports, provides a running story line that can be updated regularly, and conforms to norms regarding what constitutes balanced coverage. As a result, the partisan rhetoric on the Hill is only amplified by the news media, who track the successes and setbacks of each party, presenting political elites as polarized forces. Day-to-day and week-to-week, reporters document the compromises, concessions, roadblocks, and strategies employed by lawmakers on either side of the aisle. Factual information about the contents of a given bill is provided within this framework of partisan conflict and strategic maneuvering.

All the while, members of the public wait for a resolution to their problem. They follow the news about the debate, hoping to learn how the plan taking shape in Washington will help people like them. What they learn from the news coverage of the debate is that lawmakers cannot find common ground. Everyone in Washington seems to have lost sight of the problem at hand and to be pursuing policies designed for their own political gain. Special interests, rather than the interests of the common Joe and Jane are shaping the policy. And the tenor of the debate has deteriorated into a partisan brawl.

With their problem still unresolved and lawmakers wasting time on needless, ineffectual debate, members of the public become frustrated and deeply unsettled by the inability of lawmakers to work together. Many start to see the debate as ridiculous and disgusting rather than productive and healthy. These negative attitudes toward the policy-making process quickly become inextricably linked in people's minds with the policy itself. When they think about the policy they can't help but think about the partisan battle being waged over it—and this association tarnishes their view of the policy itself. As the debate drags on and reporters continue to offer blow-by-blow coverage of the fight, the association of the policy with the ugly process used to produce it grows stronger. As a result, public opposition to the policy mounts. By the time a resolution comes (in the form of a bill's passage or ultimate defeat), the public's patience is exhausted, and its focus has often turned to a new problem.

Fig. 1.1 provides a visual summary of this sequence of events. The theory boils down to four key elements: (1) the presence of policy debate in Washington, which (2) generates news reports on the policy-making process, which (3) leads to negative public sentiment toward the policy-making process. Lastly, because negative conceptions about the law-making process become linked to the policy itself in people's minds, the

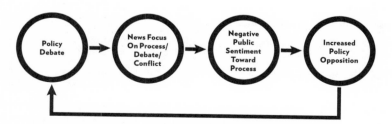

FIG. 1.1. Causal Process Leading to Increased Policy Opposition.

end result of this chain of events is decreased support and increased opposition to the policy at hand.

This process is self-reinforcing. Strategic politicians who oppose the
legislation understand that prolonging debate can work in their favor.
An incentive exists for the opposition to use parliamentary maneuvers
(like the filibuster) to stall the progress of the bill, which in turn provides
fodder for the news media, leading to more process coverage, more negative sentiment about the process, and a further increase in policy opposition. The time dynamic is, therefore, one of great importance. The longer the time span between the introduction of the bill and its ultimate
passage (or defeat), the longer the system shown here remains a closed,
self-reinforcing one. Only a conclusion to the debate can break the cycle.

This creates perverse incentives for lawmakers in the minority party.
Those who want to stymie the majority party's legislative agenda have
an incentive to generate controversy around the majority's proposals—
even when (and perhaps especially when) the substance of the legislation
is publicly popular. Doing so generates media attention focused on the
political conflict as opposed to the popular substance of the legislation.
This coverage can dampen public support for the proposal at the center
of the debate, reinforcing the minority party's commitment to conflict.
The incentives that motivate reporters and lawmakers, thus, predictably
reinforce each other's behavior, creating a feedback loop.

For the remainder of this chapter I attend to unpacking this dynamic
process. I pay particular attention to the motives that drive news reporters and the cognitive processes that underscore opinion formation. The
theory developed applies to a wide range of policies including health
care, social welfare, economic, and morality policies and it transcends
more simplistic partisan explanations of public opposition to major proposals. The hypotheses derived from the theory developed here are then
tested throughout the book via multiple methods including analysis of
media coverage, individual level experiments, aggregate analyses, and
case studies of specific policies.

If It Bleeds, It Leads

The old adage that violence, war, and crime sell newspapers remains as
true today as ever. It is not surprising, then, that political reporting is

rife with war metaphors. Physical violence rarely breaks out among lawmakers, but, judging from news reports, verbal assault is an everyday occurrence on Capitol Hill. Reports about policy making describe conflicts among lawmakers in gory detail as a way of attracting attention to an otherwise bloodless sport. Headlines allude to battles among political elites and highlight the strategies employed by those on opposite sides of the fight.

This type of conflict-focused reporting is so common that communications scholars have classified it as one of a handful of "generic news frames" employed by journalists (de Vreese 2002).[1] These frames provide reporters with templates for synthesizing complex information in ways that are routine and manageable for both the writer and the reader. The "conflict frame," which bears similarity to the "strategic" frame and "game schema," is a generic frame with a narrative structure that presents actors as polarized forces (Neuman, Just, and Crigler 1992). Reports that employ the frame focus on which side is winning and losing, and often include language related to war, competition, and games (Capella and Jamieson 1996; Jamieson 1992; Neuman et al. 1992; Patterson 1993).

Scholars have documented the conflict frame's frequent use in campaign coverage and posit that it likely dominates public affairs reporting more generally (Capella and Jamieson 1997; Morris and Clawson 2005; Patterson 1993; Zaller 1999).[2] This assumption is based on an understanding of the goals and incentives that motivate journalists. Like politicians—whose primary goal is to attract voters—the primary goal of journalists is to attract an audience (Zaller 1999). Achieving this goal has become more difficult for traditional news outlets over the past few decades owing to increased competition from the proliferation of soft news, online news, and cable news sources. The greater this competition, the more newsmakers seek to tailor their products to the preferences of their target audiences (Postman 1985; Zaller 1999). And what audiences want is not hard news, but entertainment (e.g., Bennett 1996; Graber 1984; Iyengar, Norpoth, Hanh 2004; Neuman 1991; Postman 1985; Zaller 1999). By emphasizing conflict—a key ingredient in film, television, literature, and sports—journalists are able to increase the entertainment value of public affairs reports (Iyengar, Norpoth, Hanh 2004; Zaller 1999). Yet, in so doing, journalists are also able to uphold professional norms of objectivity and to offer "balanced" coverage.

Journalistic Norms

News reporters seek to provide objective portrayals of the events and opinions they cover. To do so, they rely on professional norms and regularized procedures in gathering and reporting the news. One such norm, often referred to as indexing, is the practice of reflecting opinions in relation to how widely they are expressed by political elites (Bennett 1990; Hallin 1984; Kuklinski and Sigelman 1992). Objectivity is, therefore, predicated upon reporting all *sides* of an issue, not upon reporting the *facts*, as the relevant facts in a policy debate might be subjective.

Interviews with journalists support these assertions. When asked what they believe constitutes objectivity in news reporting, a plurality of American journalists (39%) stated "expressing fairly the position of each side in a political dispute" (Patterson 2007, 29). Another 10% stated "an equally thorough questioning of the position of each side in a political dispute" (Patterson 2007, 29). Together, 49% of the journalists surveyed stressed the importance of gathering and reporting information from elites on both sides of a political debate. Just 28% stated that "going beyond the statements of the contending sides to the hard facts of a political dispute" constitutes objectivity, and 14% gave other responses (Patterson 2007, 29). By structuring reports around the two sides of the story, the conflict frame coheres to this norm of balanced reporting.

Focusing on the competition between political actors also allows journalists to craft a running story line that can be updated regularly (Patterson 1993). The same cannot be said for reports that focus on the policy platforms of candidates or the provisions of pending legislation. Politicians stumping for a policy or for election are coached to stay "on message" by emphasizing and reemphasizing key talking points (Patterson 1993). As a result, daily (or hourly) news reports focused on the substance of these appeals would be extremely monotonous. Focusing instead on the dynamic, often contentious process of policy making allows journalists to craft reports that are fresh each day. These process stories evaluate how politician's messages are being received by the public, which candidate or lawmaker is polling ahead, and what strategies could be used to improve the fortunes of the underdog.

For all of these reasons, conflict is an essential determinant of an event's newsworthiness. But this relentless focus on conflict sometimes leads reporters to offer the public a skewed depiction of lawmaking. For instance, Eric Montpetit (2016) shows that when covering lawmaking, reporters focus on the opinions of a few "celebrity politicians or other highly visible individuals taking unexpected positions—sometimes extreme ones" (5). Other actors, who are central to the policy-making process but whose views and tactics are less extreme—such as bureaucrats and nongovernmental experts—are absent from media portrayals of the debate. By excluding the views of these more moderate actors and focusing on the most controversial aspects of the debate, the news media magnify the disagreement. As Montpetit puts it, "the disagreements covered by the media are so out of proportion that they can only inspire a strong sense of disapproval among citizens" (2016, 5).

Numerous authors who find that citizens have negative reactions to the political conflicts they learn about from the news media share this conclusion. Jacobs and Shapiro (2000) use aggregate level survey data to show that media coverage of "polarized policy struggle" generates public uncertainty about the reforms and a sense that "their personal well-being is threatened" by it (27). Cappella and Jamieson (1996) use an experimental design to demonstrate that campaign coverage focused on strategy and political tactics results in higher levels of cynicism among study participants than does coverage concentrating on policy issues. In another experimental study, Forgette and Morris (2006) show that "conflict-laden television coverage decreases public evaluations of political institutions, trust in leadership, and overall support for political parties and the system as a whole" (447). Durr, Gilmour, and Wolbrecht (1997) couple survey data with content analysis to demonstrate that periods of heightened conflict in Congress and the reflection of that conflict in the news have a negative impact on Congressional approval. In the context of campaign advertisements, a number of studies find that exposure to negativity and incivility decreases turnout (Kahn and Kenney 1999), political trust (Lau, Sigelman, and Rovner 2007; Mutz and Reeves 2005), and feelings of political efficacy (Ansolabehere and Iyengar 1995; Lau et al. 2007).[3] Members of the public may be entertained by partisan battles, but this evidence collectively suggests that they are simultaneously sickened by it.

Why Americans Love to Hate Political Conflict

Hibbing and Theiss-Morse (2002) argue that these types of negative responses to policy debate occur because many Americans view debate as politically motivated bickering that stands in the way of real problem solving. Americans generally believe there is consensus around the goals government should pursue—like a strong economy, low crime, and quality education—and think lawmakers should "just select the best way of bringing about these end goals without wasting time and needlessly exposing people to politics" (Hibbing and Theiss-Morse 2002, 133). The fact that a best solution may not be apparent or available does not occur to some members of the public. Particularly among those with lower levels of political knowledge and weaker policy preferences, "people equate the presence of dissenting policy proposals with the presence of special interests and the attendant demotion of the true consensual, general interest" (Hibbing and Theiss-Morse 2002, 157).

Political elites and members of the press further the idea that debate is unneeded and unhealthy for a democracy. A ready example comes from public discussion of Standard & Poor's decision to downgrade the United States' credit rating in 2011. The downgrade came after Democrats and Republicans ended weeks of heated deliberation over deficit reduction by agreeing to legislation that slashed government spending and increased the nation's debt ceiling. The agency's decision to downgrade the nation's debt, therefore, came after a compromise was reached and the threat of a government default had passed. Standard and Poor's instead cited "the difficulties in bridging the gulf between the political parties," as a primary concern in the report they released on August 5 (Swann 2011, 2). The report went on to say that intense partisan debate led the agency to question the "effectiveness, stability, and predictability of American policymaking and political institutions" (Swann 2011, 2). President Obama echoed these concerns in his remarks about the downgrade:

> On Friday, we learned that the United States received a downgrade by one of the credit rating agencies—not so much because they doubt our ability to pay our debt if we make good decisions, but because after witnessing a month of wrangling over raising the debt ceiling, they doubted our political system's ability to act. . . . So it's not a lack of plans or policies that's the problem here. It's a lack of political will in Washington. It's the insistence on drawing lines in the sand, a refusal to put what's best for the country ahead of self-interest or party or ideology. And that's what we need to change (Presidential Remarks 2011).

Here, the president himself asserts that partisan posturing and conflict represents "a refusal to put what's best for the country ahead of self-interest or party or ideology" (Presidential Remarks 2011). The argument that both parties might have fundamentally different views over what course is best for the country—and that public debate over which party has the better plan might be needed—was not raised.

Other examples of this attitude abound. For instance, a 2011 *Newsweek* cover was emblazoned with the headline "Let's Just Fix It!" The sub-headline touted, "Forget Washington. Move over Mr. President. Everyday Americans Can Turn This Country Around." The implication, of course, was that politicians are not serving the public interest. If average Americans were in charge, they would quickly select and implement the "best" solutions to our problems without allowing partisanship to stand in their way. Similarly, a 2012 *New Yorker* cartoon poked fun at the political process with a caption that read, "After months of partisan bickering, Congress has finally agreed to put a Slinky on an escalator and see if it goes forever" (Kanin 2012). These examples reflect the pervasive attitude that conflict and debate stand in the way of problem solving in Washington.

In sum many Americans, political elites, and members of the press view policy debate as political theater and as an impediment to problem solving. This is in part because of the public preference for cooperation between lawmakers that Hibbing and Theiss-Morse (2002) identify, in part because many Americans don't know why debate is sometimes needed, and in part because journalists concentrate on the most heated and controversial aspects of the debate (Montpetit 2016). In actuality, debate serves many functions, some of which are purely political and some of which are vital to the health of a democratic system. To be sure, politicians are always on the lookout for ways to bolster their electoral fortunes. We can expect lawmakers to call press conferences and dig in their heels when they believe taking a strong position will ingratiate them with voters, donors, or organized interests. But policy disputes also erupt when lawmakers hold sharply different views over the best course of action for the country. Contrary to public perception, the "best solution" to a complex problem is rarely self-evident. Policy making requires legislators to weigh many potential options that each have merits and drawbacks, and to speculate about future needs and resources. Lawmakers often come to different conclusions about which option is best because their preferences are guided by divergent sets of values, world-views, and predictions about the future.

A democratic process requires that such differences be aired publicly, and that citizens and members of the press be allowed to weigh in. In theory, shining sunlight on the deliberations should result in the adoption of policies that better align with public preferences, and should help minimize opportunities for government corruption. This is yet another reason why conflict is a determinant of newsworthiness; however, these legitimate reasons for public debate are seldom highlighted by the press. Instead, reporters fixate on the political ramifications of partisan contests and downplay the substantive differences at the heart of the debate. This coverage reinforces the public view that political interests rather than genuine differences of opinion motivate policy debate. As outlined above, this cynical belief then underscores negative public evaluations of the government, Congress, and the political system as a whole. In this book, I demonstrate that the media's use of the conflict frame also has predictable and important effects on individual level support for the policy proposals at the center of heated debates. Reform plans with popular provisions—like the Health Security Act, The Affordable Care Act, and No Child Left Behind—can become objects of public scorn because of their association with the unpopular, contentious process of policy making. How and why this backlash occurs is best understood as a result of the associative process of attitude formation.

The Process of Attitude Formation

The processes by which frames influence attitudes have been well documented in the cognitive psychology and political psychology literature and are grounded in the expectancy value model of attitude formation (e.g., Ajzen and Fishbein 1980; Chong and Druckman 2007; Fishbein and Hunter 1964; Nelson et al. 1997b). Very simply stated, this model describes attitude formation as a process that aggregates across the mix of information an individual associates with a given target (like a policy, a political figure, or a government institution). All things being equal, if the target is associated with mostly positive considerations, the individual will express an overall positive attitude toward the target. If the target is associated with mostly negative considerations, the individual will express an overall negative attitude. But all things are rarely equal. When some considerations become more salient to an individual—perhaps because they were central to a political campaign or were featured repeatedly in the news—those considerations will weigh more heavily in the individual's evaluation of the target (e.g., Fazio 2007; Lodge and Taber 2013; Zaller 1992; Zaller and Feldman 1992). And because most individuals are at least somewhat ambivalent toward most issues—meaning they hold some positive and some negative considerations in mind—this reweighting can alter the individual's overall opinion of the target (Zaller 1992; Zaller and Feldman 1992).

An example helps to demonstrate how this process works. Assume the target is the President of the United States. A given individual will associate many different pieces of information with the president—like his political affiliation, his stance on issues like taxes, human rights, the environment, and so forth, and information about his personality and leadership skills. Fig. 1.2 shows a visual representation of the associative map one individual might construct from this information about the president. In the top portion of the figure we see that some of the associated information is positive (as indicated with plus signs) and some of this information is negative (as indicated with minus signs). Our sample citizen likes that the president is a Democrat, likes the president's stance on taxes, and thinks the president has a number of positive personal traits. But this individual does not like the president's stances on the environment and human rights.

If all of these associated concepts were equally weighted (as in the top portion of fig. 1.2), the individual would form an overall positive impression of the president because positive considerations outnumber negative ones. But if a political opponent began to publicly and frequently criticize the president's stance on human rights—attracting media attention and public interest to the topic—the issue would become more salient for our sample citizen. The more salient the issue of human rights becomes, the more heavily it will weigh in his overall assessment of the president. If the topic became salient enough, negative considerations about human rights would overwhelm positive considerations about the president, and this individual would form an overall negative impression of the commander-in-chief. This situation is displayed in the bottom portion of fig. 1.2.

This is a stylized example of how framing shapes opinions. News

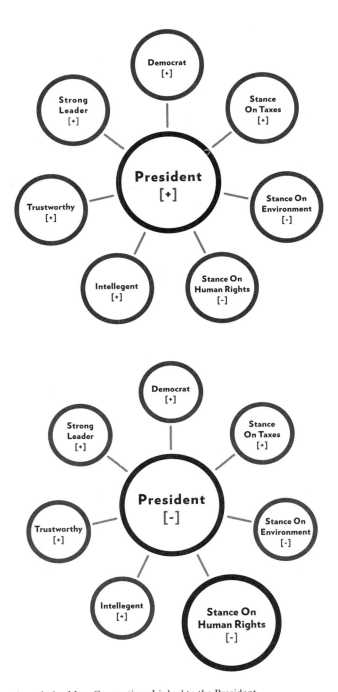

FIG. I.2. Associative Map: Conceptions Linked to the President.

frames provide "a central organizing idea" that focuses attention on one dimension of an issue or event (Gamson and Modigliani 1989, 3; also see Entman 1993). In so doing, frames elevate the salience of particular considerations and demote the salience of others—implying what information is central and what should be "left out, treated as secondary, tertiary, or less" (Cappella and Jamieson 1997, 45; also see: Druckman and Nelson 2003; Iyengar and Kinder 1987; Miller and Krosnick 2000; Nelson and Kinder 1996). By encouraging individuals to draw connections between particular concepts and heightening the salience of particular considerations, frames can shape political opinions, as demonstrated by numerous studies. Framing has been shown to shape policy preferences on a broad range of issues, including capital punishment (Baumgartner DeBoef and Boydstun 2008), the Kosovo War (Berinsky and Kinder 2006), government spending (Jacoby 2000), affirmative action (Kinder and Sanders 1990), gun policy (Haider-Markel and Joslyn 2001), public health policy (Tversky and Kahneman 1981 and 1987), and many others.

These framing effects can be limited or moderated by a number of known factors. The credibility of the source of information and the presence of competing frames can influence framing effects (e.g., Chong and Druckman 2007b; Druckman 2001). Further, individuals with strong prior attitudes have been shown to discount information that challenges them—a process known as motivated reasoning (e.g., Fischle 2000; Kim et al. 2010; Lebo and Cassino 2007; Redlawsk 2002; Taber and Lodge 2006). Individuals with strong attitudes may, therefore, be less susceptible to framing effects. Yet even with these limitations, framing can have a powerful effect on aggregate level public opinion. For instance, Frank Baumgartner and his colleagues demonstrate the role framing has played in shaping mass attitudes toward the death penalty (Baumgartner et al. 2008). The authors tracked and catalogued the frames used in news articles about capital punishment over the course of several decades. They found that, over time, public discourse on capital punishment shifted from a focus on the moral necessity of retribution to the potential innocence of the accused. These two sets of considerations support different evaluations of capital punishment—the former supports a positive evaluation of the policy while the latter supports a negative one. By heightening the salience of considerations that support a negative evaluation of the policy, the shift in framing led public support for the death penalty to diminish over time (Baumgartner et al. 2008).

The Impact of the Conflict Frame on Policy Attitudes

The conflict frame shapes opinions in a similar way by highlighting negative information about the policy-making process and obscuring information about the substance of proposed bills. As I will demonstrate in chapter 2, news reports rarely focus on the link between policy proposals and the problems they are designed to redress—information that might be viewed positively by many members of the public. As described above, journalists instead emphasize the role that proposed bills play in a larger partisan contest.

This pattern of news coverage suggests that policy debate is fundamentally a political process rather than an exercise in problem solving. And it leads many Americans to believe that lawmakers are striving to advance their own interests rather than the common good. *This is especially true for those who know less about how government works* and who do not have strong preexisting policy preference. These individuals are not married to any particular policy solution and do not have strong feelings about the provisions that would make a bill desirable or undesirable. This is in part because they have trouble understanding the relationships between specific provisions and their potential outcomes (Arnold 1990). Without a dog in the fight, people simply want lawmakers to choose a solution that will "work" and think finding one would be straightforward if lawmakers would work together. For these reasons, heated debate between lawmakers over the details of legislation seems contrived rather than legitimate to these Americans. When they turn on the evening news, they hope to hear how proposed policies will fix problems and improve their lives. Instead, they learn that Democrats and Republicans are at each other's throats. They hear how the issue will affect the upcoming elections. And they hear about parliamentary maneuvering, delays, and veto threats. In short, debate sends a clear signal (amplified by the news media) that politicians are not working to advance the common good. Instead, these individuals view policy debate as a sign that lawmakers are prioritizing their political goals and that the government is broken.

The application of the conflict frame to reports about lawmaking establishes the centrality of these negative considerations about the policy-making process to evaluations of the policies themselves. As a result, this framing has the power to shape the associative maps news consumers construct in their minds. When news coverage about a pending policy is dominated by descriptions of the tenor of the debate, the associative maps constructed by news consumers will also be dominated by these negative considerations. As shown in fig. 1.3, this means that information about the process has the potential to overwhelm substantive considerations in the formation of policy attitudes. Here, the individual has information in mind about four of the major the provisions that make up the bill under consideration—and she likes each of those provisions. But she does not like that the bill is associated with a partisan, divisive legislative process. This information about the process is highly salient, and so it dominates her associative map, leaving her with an overall negative impression of the bill. This is why individuals often reject policies that are comprised of discrete provisions they favor. Policy support is a function not only of the content of the legislation, but also of the process that produced it (as described by the news media). When the latter is more salient than the former, it will play a critical role in shaping policy opinion.

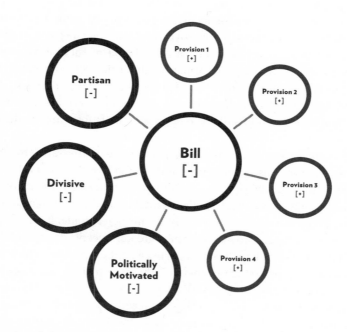

FIG. 1.3. Associative Map: Conceptions Linked to a Bill.

Political Sophistication and the Indirect Effect of Conflict

Some Americans are more knowledgeable than others about politics, the policy-making process, and the substantive details of current policy debates. These individuals, who also tend to have stronger preexisting policy opinions, constitute a minority of the public. For several reasons, they will respond differently to partisan conflict than will the less informed, average Americans described above. First, because they know more about pending legislation, political actors, and world events, the associative maps political sophisticates construct around these targets will be populated with a larger number of considerations (Zaller and Feldman 1992). With more considerations in mind, several authors find that the politically knowledgeable are less susceptible to the influence of framing effects (i.e., Feldman 1989; Iyengar 1991; Zaller 1990; Zaller and Feldman 1992).[4] As explained by Zaller and Feldman (1992), "attitude reports formed from an average of many considerations will be a more reliable indicator of the underlying population of considerations than an average based on just one or two considerations" (597).

Take, for example, the associative map displayed in fig. 1.3. If we add information about several more provisions to this map (as in fig. 1.4), negative information about the tenor of the debate (salient as it is) would no longer be able to outweigh information about the bill's substance. Having more information in mind can temper the influence of news frames and lead to attitude stability. For this reason, the mere association of a policy with conflict is less likely to depress support for it among the most knowledgeable individuals.

People who are more knowledgeable about politics are also better able to link policy issues and proposals to the liberal/conservative continuum (Converse 1964). This allows them to understand the ideological differences between discrete policy provisions and to distinguish liberal proposals from conservative ones. With this better understanding of the differences between provisions comes greater acceptance of policy debate between lawmakers. When a partisan fight erupts over which provisions to include or exclude from a bill, these individuals are more likely than others to see the conflict as a legitimate expression of ideological differences. In fact, these individuals typically view politics through an ideological lens and use ideology to structure their own political preferences and beliefs (Converse 1964). Unlike less sophisticated Americans,

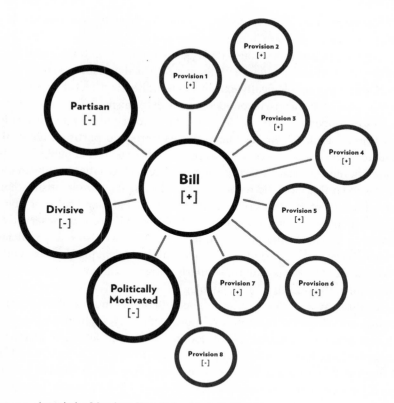

FIG. I.4. Associative Map for a Knowledgeable Individual.

these "ideologues" *are* partial to specific policy provisions and *do* have a dog in the fight. They want to see policies enacted that align with their ideological worldviews and follow debates in Washington to learn how closely proposed legislation matches up with their preferences. Ideologues then use this information to decide whether they will support new proposals.

The presence or absence of partisan conflict in Washington sends signals about a bill's ideology that these political sophisticates can use to evaluate the legislation. They will infer that bills favored by Democrats are liberal, that bills favored by Republicans are conservative, and that bills generating heated conflict between the parties are ideologically extreme. Whereas compromise between the parties would signal the bill's moderate nature, intense debate signals that the legislation is either so liberal or so conservative (depending on which party proposed it) that the parties are unable to find common ground.

Because these sophisticates form policy opinions on the basis of how closely the legislation aligns with their ideological preferences, the signal that a policy is ideologically extreme can indirectly affect their support for it. Few Americans favor ideological extremism. Most view themselves as moderates and say they would like to see more bipartisanship on Capitol Hill. When lawmakers instead produce partisan, ideologically extreme policies—or policies perceived as such—the public rejects them. In the aggregate, this rejection of extreme legislation results in the well-known thermostatic response—public calls for conservatism when the government produces policies that are too liberal and calls for liberalism when the government produces policies that are too conservative (Wlezien 1995). At the individual level, Americans also reject policies they believe are out of step with their own ideological preferences. Only individuals with views that are similarly extreme will favor bills they believe fall at the outskirts of the ideological spectrum.

In this way, the presence or absence of conflict indirectly shapes the policy opinions of those who are more politically sophisticated by influencing their placement of the legislation on the left/right ideological spectrum. For instance, suppose a Democratic bill is introduced in Congress that would increase public school funding. If the bill generated partisan conflict, strong liberals would place it closer to themselves (at the far left of the ideological spectrum) because the controversy would suggest to them that the bill is extremely liberal. Given the perceived congruence between their own preferences and the content of the bill, strong liberals would be more inclined to support the bill under such circumstances than they would if the bill generated bi-partisan support. Conservatives and moderates, on the other hand, would be less likely to support the bill if it generated controversy than they would if it received bi-partisan support. This is because the heated debate would similarly suggest to them the extremely liberal nature of the bill. Ultimately, the closer an ideologically-minded individual places a bill to him or herself on the ideological spectrum, the more likely he or she will be to support it.

Fig. 1.5 illustrates this concept visually. The top portion of the figure represents the beginning of the policy debate—time one (T_1). At this point, there has been little partisan debate. Members of the public simply know that a Democratic education bill has been introduced in Con-

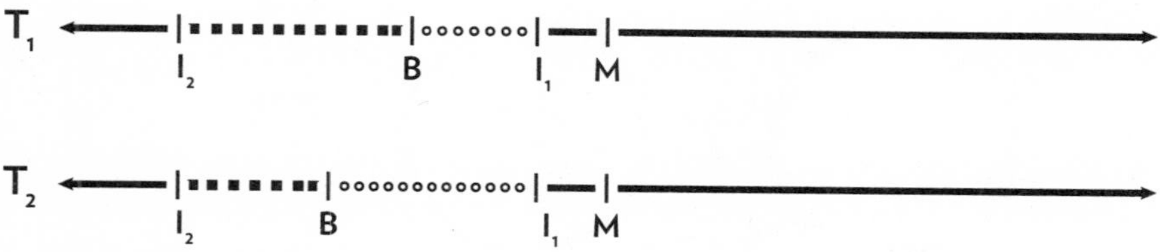

FIG. 1.5. Bill Placement on an Ideological Scale.

gress that would increase federal K-12 funding. Because the bill (B) is a Democratic one, members of the public have placed it to the left of the median (M) on the left/right ideological spectrum. This placement puts the bill fairly close to individual one (I_1), a left-leaning moderate, and relatively far from individual two (I_2), a strong liberal.

As the debate over the legislation spans weeks and months, members of the public hear more and more about the partisan conflict in Washington. They learn from the news media that the Democrats are battling the Republicans in Congress for passage of the bill. Using this information, individuals update their placement of the bill on the ideological spectrum. The result of this updating is shown in the bottom portion of fig. 1.5, which represents time two (T_2). Here, the bill is placed farther to the left than it was in time one. Because of its association with heated partisan debate, the public views the bill as being more ideologically extreme, which, in the case of this Democratic bill, means more liberal. The location of the bill is now farther from our left-leaning moderate (I_1) and closer to our strong liberal (I_2). Based on the updated placement of the bill, we should expect individual one to like the bill less than he did before the heated debate began, and individual two to like the bill more.

The Dual Influence of the Conflict Frame

In sum, the conflict frame is expected to influence policy attitudes in two ways, which are summarized by fig. 1.6. First, the conflict frame can affect policy attitudes directly, through the associative process described. When policies are linked in people's minds with negative concepts like partisanship and divisiveness, these concepts become part of the mix of information that is aggregated across in the formation of an overall attitude toward the policy. In this way, these associations can depress

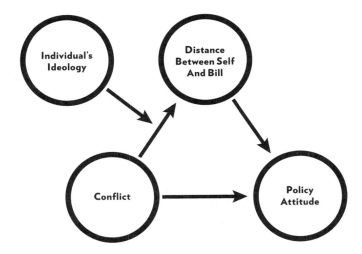

FIG. 1.6. Direct and Indirect Influence of Conflict on Policy Opinion.

support for policies at the center of a political battle. This direct effect should be most prevalent among individuals with weak preexisting policy preferences and those who know less about politics.

The conflict frame can also influence policy attitudes indirectly by altering the perceived distance between the individual and the bill on the ideological spectrum. The interaction between the individual's ideological self-placement and the ideology of the bill determines whether the association of a bill with partisan debate causes the individual to place the bill closer to or further from him or herself. But note that in the aggregate, the signal that a bill is ideologically extreme will have a negative net effect on support for it because few Americans place themselves at either extreme of the ideological spectrum. This indirect effect should be most prevalent among politically knowledgeable individuals with strong, ideologically based policy preferences.

Both of these reactions to policies associated with an adversarial lawmaking process are distinct from reactions based on partisan attitudes toward specific policies. This is not because the conflict frame does not highlight the partisan nature of legislation—it does. Reports that focus on conflict in Washington naturally emphasize partisan divisions because the two sides of the debate are typically the Democrats and the Republicans. Highlighting this divide provides a useful signal for partisans—clearly indicating which side of the issue their team is on. We might expect this cue to generate increased support among members of the party that proposed the legislation, decreased support among members of the opposition party, and to have no impact on independents. But the influence of the conflict frame goes beyond these party cues—depressing policy support across the board. I will demonstrate that, while the frame's influence is often strongest among members of the opposition party, independents are also less likely to support policies associated with conflict, and so are members of the party that proposed the divisive legislation. This makes the conflict frame a powerful rhetorical weapon that opponents can use to chip away at public support among members of the proponent's own party.

Whether its impact is direct or indirect, the news media's frequent use of the conflict frame is expected to systematically shape public policy opinion. Policies that are associated with heated partisan debate should garner less public support than they would otherwise. Further, the larger and longer the debate, the more precipitous the decline in support. This means that obstruction and timing are important, as slowing things down to extend the debate will predictably heighten support for the status quo. But this is only because the corrosive effect of the conflict frame leads to declining support for policies whose substantive goals may have broad and unchanging public support. In fact, opponents of a piece of legislation may focus their objections on the lawmaking process itself, claiming, for instance, that the bill is being pushed through Congress with parliamentary maneuvers that limit minority party input. Such arguments bypass the substance of the law altogether, focusing public attention on the strategic, combative elements of lawmaking that the public dislikes. This framing makes the legislation seem ideologically extreme and politically motivated.

Structure of this Book

Chapters 2 through 6 systematically test the hypotheses outlined here. Chapter 2 addresses the fundamental claim that the conflict frame's use is widespread in public affairs reports. Unlike previous studies that have focused primarily on the frame's use in campaign coverage, my analysis in chapter 2 reports about policy proposals and the societal problems those proposals seek to address. It relies on an original dataset of full-text articles published in the *New York Times* between 1980 and 2010 and employs content analysis to assess the degree to which the conflict frame is used therein. Whereas political blogs, talk radio shows, and cable news reports are known to highlight conflict (and even to generate it) (Sobieraj and Barry 2011), elite newspapers should be less likely to do so. The *New York Times*, in particular, is an elite newspaper with an established readership and a staff of highly trained journalists. As such, it should be among the news outlets that are least likely to exploit political conflict for a boost in readership. If there is widespread use of the conflict frame in *NYT* reports, its use is likely widespread throughout the news industry.

I find that descriptions of conflict are ubiquitous in policy-focused news reports. Seventy percent of the policy-focused articles sampled contained descriptions of parliamentary tactics, political strategies, partisan debate, or heated confrontations between political elites. Forty-nine percent contained descriptions of two or more of these contentious aspects of the policy-making process. In contrast, just 32% of reports were focused on the substantive details of policies under consideration. Moreover, articles that describe pending legislation seldom give significant attention to the societal problems these proposals were meant to ameliorate. Policy problems and solutions are typically discussed separately. And unlike policy-focused articles, fewer than 20% of the articles that focus on societal problems highlight conflict. Instead, the majority of these articles focus on the substance of the problem. When problem-focused articles are embellished to add interest, it is typically with descriptions of the individuals and communities affected by particular problems.[5]

Articles that discuss societal problems could be framed in terms of conflict and, in fact, some are. A small subset of the problem-focused articles outlined debates over the causes and severity of social ills like poverty and homelessness, discussing who is responsible for these problems and who ought to fix them. But far more often, debate and conflict were not part of the dialogue about societal problems until the discussion entered the arena of government action. Once within that arena, the conflicts highlighted were, most often, those of a political nature. This pattern of news coverage, which uncouples problems and solutions, helps to explain American's negative perceptions of policy debate. Because news reports do not focus on the link between policy proposals and the problems they are designed to redress, conflict over public policy does not seem to be aimed at problem solving. Instead, proposals that are heavily debated seem designed to advance political goals because they are described in terms of their role in a larger partisan conflict.

The rest of the book focuses on the effects of this framing on public policy opinion. Chapter 3 uses two experiments (one with student data and one with a national sample) to assess the impact of the conflict frame on individual-level policy support. In both experiments, study participants read a short vignette describing a proposed education policy. The vignettes were modeled after real *New York Times* articles and each includes identical information about the substance of the policy. All of the vignettes also describe the particular elements of the bill about which Republicans and Democrats disagree. The treatments differ in their descriptions of the tenor of the debate—the "conflict" treatments describe the process as a "partisan brawl" while the "civil debate" treatments describe lawmakers working to resolve their differences.

The experimental design is particularly useful because it allows me to compare support for a partisan proposal with support for a bipartisan one. In the real world, bipartisan proposals typically receive little news coverage and are rarely the subject of polling questions, making it hard to measure support for them with observational data. However, bipartisan bills are quite common on Capitol Hill. In chapter 6, I show that from 1981 to 2012, there were just as many major enactments passed with overwhelming bipartisan support as with slim partisan majorities. The experiment allows me to assess how members of the public would respond to these bipartisan enactments if they knew more about them.

Both experiments show that policies associated with heated conflict are viewed as more ideologically extreme than are identical policies not associated with heated conflict. Further, the perceived distance between the bill's ideology and the participant's ideology is a significant predictor of policy support—especially among political sophisticates. The further these participants placed the bill from themselves on a seven-point ideological scale, the less likely they were to support it. This finding provides evidence of the indirect effect of conflict on policy support; however, even when controlling for this ideological component, support for the policy is lower among participants given one of the "conflict treatments." The presence of heated debate does more than just send a signal about the relative extremism of the policy under consideration. It also signals dysfunction in the political process. This signal is particularly consequential for individuals who are *not* political sophisticates. Using the national sample (which comes from the 2012 Cooperative Congres-

sional Election Study), I find that individuals with lower levels of political knowledge are the most susceptible to the influence of the conflict
frame when estimates of the bill's ideology are controlled for. These individuals dislike policies associated with conflict, regardless of their substantive provisions. In the remainder of the book, I focus primarily on
this direct effect of conflict on policy attitudes.

The results of the experiments provide support for my theory but
they leave questions about generalizability and external validity unresolved. To address these questions, I employ a quasi-experimental design in the fourth chapter to supply evidence from the "real word" that
bolsters the experimental findings. Here, I examine support for the Federal Marriage Amendment (FMA) in 2004 and 2005—a period during
which fifteen states considered ballot measures on constitutional amendments banning same-sex marriage. Residents of those states found themselves at the center of an emotionally charged debate and were the targets of well-funded campaigns vying for ballot measure votes. Residents
of states without such campaigns encountered demonstrably less debate
about gay marriage. This allows for a comparison of attitudes toward the
FMA among residents of states experiencing high versus low levels of
political conflict.

Using national survey data collected in March of 2004 and April of
2005, I show that support for the FMA fell markedly in ballot-measure
states but remained stable in other states over the course of the debate.
In fact, results from a logit model show that support for the FMA fell
among residents of ballot measure states even when controlling for the
respondents' underlying attitudes toward the legalization of gay marriage (the crux of the policy's substantive provisions). Further analysis
shows that support for and opposition to the legalization of gay marriage
remained constant over the same period. Residents of ballot measure
states did not become more tolerant of same-sex marriage over time.
Instead, they became increasingly frustrated with a divisive policy that
they began to view as a politically motivated, wedge issue.

Unlike the case of gay marriage described in chapter 4, many of the
policy debates that capture public attention center on proposed laws that
are complex and multifaceted. Health care reform is just such a complex
issue, one that has appeared on the political agendas of almost every
president to serve since the end of the Second World War. In chapter 4
I develop two parallel health policy case studies. The first focuses on the
failed Clinton health care reforms and the second focuses on the Obama

health care reforms. I examine how the debates were respectively portrayed in the press, and the disconnect between the public's support for the substance of the two bills and its opposition to the reform packages as a whole.

Qualitative and quantitative approaches are used to show that in both cases, the media's focus on the contentious lawmaking process led many members of the public to believe legislators were pursuing their own political interests rather than the public good. I then examine the factors that shaped public opposition to both policies in detail using national survey data. Regression results show that for individuals with lower levels of political sophistication, the belief that lawmakers were "playing politics" dramatically increased the likelihood of opposition to both the Clinton plan and the Affordable Care Act. These findings are robust even when controlling for partisanship and attitudes toward the main substantive provisions of the two bills.

In chapter 6, I ask how the news media and public respond when the policy-making process is a *bi*partisan one. I provide evidence of a clear selection effect in which reporters devote roughly five times more coverage to important laws enacted by a slim majority as compared with those enacted by a large, bipartisan coalition. Further, I use aggregate-level survey data to show that nearly unanimous enactments are more popular with the public than are contentious laws. Finally, I show that contentious policies typically shed supporters over time using aggregate-level survey data.

The findings provided in chapters 2 through 6 show that conflict between lawmakers and the media's portrayal of that conflict depresses public support for policies with popular substantive provisions. They also raise questions about the relationship between media coverage, policy debate, and the public's attitude toward the government itself. The news media systematically focus their attention on policies that generate controversy among elites and frame that coverage as a competition between lawmakers. Policies that are equally important and widely popular (among politicians and members of the public) receive scant coverage. This selection effect leaves citizens with a distorted view of their government. The widespread use of the conflict frame means that Americans are all too aware of disagreements between lawmakers, but receive little information about the many instances of compromise and cooperation on Capitol Hill. I explore the relationship between contentious debate, policy support, trust in government, and presidential approval in the concluding chapter.

CHAPTER TWO

The Dominance of the "Conflict Frame"

"I mean, the fact that the C.B.O. acknowledges that we could give all Americans health care, and that we will in fact lower health care expenditures in the long run, and that it's ultimately going to lead to deficit reduction. . . . I sure as hell hope that this kind of in-the-beltway scorekeeping issue is not used as a weapon to kill health care reform." —Leon E. Panetta, Director of the Office of Management and Budget (Clymer 1994)

Reports that describe a policy debate in Washington can be framed many ways. Sometimes they are dry and factual, detailing the provisions of the plan along with its estimated costs and benefits. More often, however, reports focus on the process of lawmaking rather than the substance of the proposed law. These process stories chronicle who is winning and losing the partisan battle for passage of the bill as well as the tactics employed by those on either side of the fight. As Leon Panetta indicates in the quote above, this type of coverage can damage public perceptions of the legislation under debate.

News reports that highlight the partisan nature of the policy-making process focus public attention on conflicts between lawmakers. These conflicts seem petty to some members of the public, many of whom do not have strong policy preferences (e.g., Converse 1964; Zaller 1992). Without a dog in the fight, average Americans just want to see Congress select the "best" solution to the problem at hand—whatever that policy may be (Hibbing and Theiss-Morse 2002). When agreement on the best solution cannot be reached, some Americans believe it is because lawmakers are working to advance their own political interests rather than the public interest.

An example helps to illustrate why some Americans see policy debate as a sign that lawmakers have lost sight of the problems confronting the nation. In 2001, the national news media covered an array of issues related to school safety and performance. Reports in the *New York Times* described increased incidents of school bullying, inadequate textbooks, overcrowded schools, low teacher pay, and insufficient teacher training. Most of these articles about problems in education were focused on the findings of recently published studies and were reported in a "just the facts" sort of way. Take, for example, the following three excerpts from articles published in the *Times* during 2001:

Twelve of the most popular science textbooks used in middle schools across the nation are riddled with errors, a two-year study led by a North Carolina State University researcher has found (*New York Times* 2001).

Threats, ridicule, name calling, hitting, slapping and other forms of intimidation and harassment are a common feature of life in America's classrooms, researchers have found, in the first large-scale national study of bullying in the schools (Goode 2001).

Teachers in the United States earn less relative to national income than their counterparts in many industrialized countries, yet they spend far more hours in front of the classroom, according to a major new international study (Wilgoren 2001).

These straightforward descriptions of problems in schools made the problems themselves seem self-evident. The articles were written in a style that suggested all Americans should agree that errors in textbooks, bullying, and low teacher pay were major problems confronting our nation's welfare. And, in fact, many did come to see these issues as major problems and to believe that the government should find solutions to them. So when President G. W. Bush took office in 2001, education reform topped his domestic agenda.

With unified Republican control of the House and Senate, as well as pledges from Congressional Democrats to work with the Bush Administration, the overall political climate around the issue of education reform was one of bipartisanship. Democrats George Miller and Edward Kennedy even signed on to the president's "No Child Left Behind" plan as cosponsors. Yet even under these cooperative conditions, news coverage of the reform plan often highlighted the few areas of disagreement between the Democrats and Republicans:

A Senate committee today unanimously approved a crucial education bill embodying President Bush's calls for changes in education, but several committee Democrats threatened to withdraw their support if the administration did not back a substantial increase in spending for schools in poor areas (Schemo 2001).

After a morning meeting on the issue, Democrats agreed they should continue to fight for more money, arguing that the federal government was not meeting its financial obligations to the nation's poorest schools. . . . Senate Republicans argued that money was not a cure-all and accused Democrats of stalling to pressure President Bush (Alvarez 2001a).

Democrats are still battling the White House over how much money the federal government should send to schools with poor and disabled children, an issue that could ultimately undermine the bill (Alvarez 2001b).

These discussions about the bill's chances for passage, the areas of disagreement between the parties, the use of delay tactics, and so forth gobbled up column inches that could alternatively have been devoted to descriptions of the bill's provisions—many of which were very popular. Table 2.1 shows that annual testing, increased teacher training, and plans to hold schools accountable for student achievement were favored by more than 70% of the public. Focusing on these aspects of the legislation would not only have highlighted areas of agreement (between lawmakers and between members of the public), but would also have created an opportunity to discuss how the legislation proposed to solve many of the problems facing America's schools.

This is the information most Americans say they want from the news—an explanation of how legislation will affect people like themselves and resolve problems. It is also information that many Americans believe the news media does a poor job of providing (e.g., Times Mirror 1995; Pew 2009b; Pew 2010b). The focus on the policy-making process, as opposed to policy substance, obscures the problem solving aspect of lawmaking—making it hard for observers to figure out how the policy will correct the societal problem it is supposed to redress.[1] In fact, many Americans may not see the policy as an attempt to correct a prob-

TABLE 2.1. **Support for the Substantive Provisions of NCLB.**

Provision	Support	Oppose
PSRA/Newsweek Poll, February 2001		
Regular student testing in math and English. Reward schools that show improved test scores with increased federal funding.	73%	22%
Los Angeles Times Poll, March 2001		
Retrain teachers in reading instruction for students in K–3, annual testing in math and science, hold schools accountable for progress.	80%	15%
Gallup, June 2001		
Hold the public schools accountable for how much students learn.	75%	20%

lem at all because it is simply not portrayed that way by the news media. As I will demonstrate, policy problems and solutions are discussed separately in the news—and while problems are treated as something we can all agree on—solutions are treated as fodder for political sniping. As a result, many news consumers believe that the public is unified in its preference for a "good" solution, which should be as self-evident as the problem at hand. When lawmakers are seen "bickering" over policy proposals, many Americans believe they are not attempting to address societal problems at all, but are instead engaging in policy debates designed to advance partisan, political interests.

The greater the news media focus on the horse race, legislative tactics, incivility, and partisanship associated with a policy, the larger this negative sentiment grows among members of the public. This makes the amount of time between a bill's introduction, passage, and implementation critical. With bipartisan support, a bill can be proposed, passed, and implemented quickly. But more often, the initial bipartisan agreement that something must be done is eroded by a partisan dispute over what exactly will be done. When these negotiations between the parties drag on for months or years, the stakes increase and the debate becomes more heated as the amount of political capital expended by the major players mounts. The news media magnify this heightened partisanship (Jacobs and Shapiro 2000; Montpetit 2016), and public support for the policy shrinks in response.

Here again, debate surrounding No Child Left Behind provides a ready example. By the time NCLB entered the implementation and reauthorization phases, the bipartisanship that surrounded the bill's initial passage had vaporized. Major disagreements erupted between Democrats and Republicans, and between federal and local education officials regarding how best to put the plan into effect. In covering the policy's implementation, the news media focused on the most sensational aspects of these disagreements:

> The Education Department sent a blistering warning to school commissioners across the country today, calling educators who try to sidestep the intent of President Bush's signature education act, No Child Left Behind, "enemies of equal justice and equal opportunity," and vowing, "they will not succeed" (Schemo 2002).

> Education Secretary Rod Paige said Monday that the National Education Association, one of the nation's largest labor unions, was like "a terrorist organization" because of the way it was resisting many provisions of a school improvement law pushed through Congress by President Bush in 2001 (Pear 2004).

As the debate dragged on and grew more heated, the amount of attention it received from the news media swelled. A LexisNexis search shows the policy was mentioned in fifty-eight *New York Times* articles during the legislative session in which it passed with bipartisan support. In the session that followed, which was punctuated by heated disputes over the plan's implementation, the *New York Times* ran four hundred articles about the NCLB. As the excerpts above illustrate, these articles often highlighted ugly, partisan conflicts between political elites.

Public reaction to the conflict over the NCLB and the portrayal of that conflict by the press was negative. As described in a report on NCLB from the Brookings Institution, "The American public initially favored NCLB by a comfortable margin, but polls from 2001 to 2005 show opponents steadily gaining on the law's supporters. In 2005, sentiments were evenly divided" (Loveless 2006).

Examples like this one abound and help to illustrate the theory I advance here. They demonstrate the media's fixation on elite conflict (even when the broader story is one of cooperation), the escalation in elite rhetoric that occurs when policy debates are prolonged, and the attrition of public support that results from exposure to this conflict.

To move from example to evidence, I begin systematically unpacking this process by analyzing the content of policy-focused and problem-focused news stories. I show that societal problems and policy solutions are typically discussed in separate reports and that unlike problem-focused articles, articles that discuss policy proposals frequently employ a "conflict frame." I argue that these patterns of coverage are the result of professional norms and routines followed by journalists, which I describe in detail in the next section. This analysis lays the groundwork for the remainder of this book, which provides an in-depth study of the effects of exposure to this reporting on public policy opinions.

Norms in News Reporting

The news media play an integral role in the democratic system. Individuals must rely on news outlets for information about the actions of the government because most are not able to directly observe the behavior of lawmakers. Even in an age of C-SPAN and a digitized Congressional Record, few citizens have the time and motivation needed to keep track of lawmaking using primary sources. The task of following, filtering, organizing, and digesting huge amounts of political information for public consumption falls to journalists. As they perform this task, public affairs reporters prioritize the dissemination of information that citizens need to evaluate their elected representatives (Shoemaker and Reese 1996). As journalists select and package this information, the incentives and professional norms that govern their industry shape the news in important ways.

One norm that shapes the news is the way that journalists classify events and issues as either "hard" or "soft" news. Events that occur within the confines of government institutions (like the introduction of a bill, the election of a president, or the handing down of a court ruling) are classified as "hard news," reflecting the primacy of information relevant to the evaluation of government actors (Tuchman 1978). These reports are assigned to reporters who cover particular "beats" (like politics or foreign affairs) and are held to the highest standards of objectivity. In addition to treating both sides of a debate fairly (Patterson 2007), journalists reporting hard news must avoid literary and cinematographic conventions that are associated with fiction. For instance, in televised hard news reports, footage of people and events is typically shown in real-time using a straight-on camera angle to indicate the factual nature of the report (Tuchman 1978). Conversely, reports focused on aspects of the human experience are classified as "soft news" and are typically covered by "features" reporters, "style" reporters or the equivalent. Soft news reports offer more room for creativity in terms of the styles of writing and cinematographic effects deemed appropriate (Tuchman 1978).

The norms used to distinguish hard news from soft news items leads to the expectation that societal problems and policy solutions will be discussed separately by the news media. While policy making takes place within the confines of government institutions (making it hard news), society itself is the venue wherein societal problems unfold (making them soft news). Reports that focus on the connection between problems and potential governmental solutions represent a hybrid form of news report that falls into a gray area between hard and soft. As is often the case when a task falls outside traditional jurisdictional boundaries, such articles are less likely to be written. In fact, in an analysis of news reports about health policy, Jacobs and Shapiro (2000) treat conflict-focused reporting and problem-focused reporting as mutually exclusive news frames and find that conflict coverage supplants news coverage of national problems. During periods when the news media focus heavily on conflicts between lawmakers, fewer articles devoted to societal problems are published. All of this evidence underscores the first hypothesis tested in this chapter:

> **H1:** Societal problems and policy solutions will be discussed in separate news reports.

A second norm that shapes the news is the reliance of reporters on familiar frames. Media frames "organize the presentation of facts and opinions within a newspaper article or television news story" (Nelson, Clawson and Oxley 1997a). The handful of media frames that reporters regularly draw on—sometimes called "generic" or "journalistic frames"—provide reporters with a template for synthesizing complex information. Neuman, Just, and Crigler (1992) identify five such frames in an analysis of newspaper, news magazine, and television news stories. Those frames are the following:

1. The economic frame, which "reflects the preoccupation with 'the bottom line,' profit and loss, and wider values of the culture of capitalism" (63).

2. The conflict frame, which focuses on "polarized forces—'the two sides of the issue'" (64).
3. The powerlessness frame, which describes individuals or groups "as helpless in the face of greater forces" (67).
4. The human impact frame, which "focuses on describing individuals and groups who are likely to be affected by an issue" (69).
5. The morality frame, which generally contains indirect references to moral and cultural values (72).

Any topic of public concern could conceivably be presented using one of these five frames. However, the need to attract readers and the desire to employ standards of objectivity make certain generic frames more likely to be used in conjunction with hard versus soft news. As I outlined in the introduction, the conflict frame adds an element of entertainment to public affairs reports and allows journalists to craft a narrative that can be regularly updated. This framing helps to enliven subject matter that might otherwise seem dull and dry to most Americans. In so doing, journalists attract readers while also respecting norms of objectivity. The frame's focus on "polarized forces" allows journalists to craft reports that give "balanced" coverage to the two sides of the story. Because the frame allows journalists to achieve the twin goals of attracting readers and employing objective standards, the conflict frame is expected to be widely used in hard news reports.

The economic frame might also be applicable to hard news reports—particularly those about policy making. This frame focuses on "profits and loss" (Neuman et al. 1992, 64). Applying it to reports about lawmaking would allow for a discussion of the policy's likely impact on the economy or a discussion of how much the policy would cost (or save) the government. This is important information that citizens can use to evaluate the merits of legislation and the lawmakers who support it. The application of the economic frame to reports about policy making could, therefore, help journalists achieve the goal of providing information needed for the evaluation of government actors.

Other frames are less likely to be used in hard news reports. For instance, the human impact frame (like Iyengar's [1992] "episodic frame") describes the effect of an event on particular individuals.[2] This necessitates a somewhat one-sided treatment of the issue at hand, which is difficult to reconcile with the requirement that hard news reports treat both sides of a debate fairly. Likewise, the powerlessness frame's portrayal of groups or individuals as "helpless in the face of greater forces" requires the reporter to single out particular "forces" as oppressive (Neuman et al. 1992, 67). By making this type of value judgment, journalists may run afoul of the norms of objectivity required for hard news reports. In contrast, these frames pose less of a problem for soft news reports. Because the subject matter of soft news is the human experience, frames that focus on the experiences of groups and individuals seem a natural fit. Further, because these reports are not held to the same strict standards of objectivity, journalists have more latitude to employ the human impact and powerlessness frames in soft news reports. This leads to two additional hypotheses:

H2: The conflict frame will be used more frequently in reports about public policy than will other frames.

H3: The conflict frame will be used less often in reports about societal problems than will other frames.

Ultimately, the selection of a particular news frame structures both the content of the report and the way the public views the underlying issue. Articles that employ the conflict frame elevate the salience of information about disputes between lawmakers while simultaneously demoting the salience of information about the substance of the proposals. In this way, the frame's use obscures the policy's potential for problem solving. To demonstrate this, I use content analysis to establish the widespread use of the conflict frame in articles focused on policy making and the frame's limited use in articles concentrating on societal problems. I also examine the quantity and placement of substantive information that describes the content of proposed legislation. Later on, I explore the impact of this framing on public policy opinion.

Creation of the News Database

To test the hypotheses outlined above, I analyzed the content of *New York Times* articles in three broad areas of domestic policy: health care, K through 12 education, and social welfare. Using a set of keywords described in Appendix A, I downloaded from LexisNexis the full text of every article on one of these topics published between January of 1980 and December of 2010. This included both hard and soft news reports, ensuring that I would collect articles that addressed both societal problems and policy solutions. I then coded a 10% sample of the health and welfare databases and a 20% sample of the smaller education dataset. In all, 831 policy- and problem-focused articles were coded through a process of human text annotation.[3]

There are two primary reasons for the selection of these particular policy areas. First, domestic problems and programs impact citizens directly, whereas international affairs can seem more abstract to average Americans. As a result, Americans are typically more interested in, more knowledgeable about, and have stronger opinions on domestic issues than they do on international ones (e.g., Delli-Carpini and Keeter 1996; Holsti 2004). I focus primarily on domestic policy topics for precisely these reasons. To bolster the claim that news framing systematically shapes public opinion, I have selected issue areas on which Americans have relatively stronger, more stable opinions.

Additionally, I have selected these topics because testing the hypothesis that the conflict frame is widely used in public affairs reports required that I cast a wide net. Had I focused on a single, narrow policy topic, such as Medicare reform or the school lunch program, my ability to generalize beyond those policy areas would be limited. In contrast, the issue areas selected cover a wide range of the topics and programs that regularly come before Congress. The health category, for instance, includes articles that focus on a range of topics, including (but not limited to) the cost of health care in the US; threats to public health; health policy initiatives and reforms; appropriations and budget requests for Medicaid, Medicare, and CHIP; innovations in medicine; and the causes, effects, and treatment of particular diseases and disorders. Similarly, the education category includes articles that pertain to a broad set of issues, including school funding disparities, education choice programs, high school dropout prevention, standards and pay for public school teachers, federal spending on preschool through grade 12 education, student discipline, violence in schools, student nutrition, and disparities in educational outcomes. Finally, the welfare database includes articles on a broad range of topics, including budget requests and reform proposals for means tested programs; the effectiveness of federal and state public assistance programs; the problems of poverty, hunger and homelessness; and discussions of the inadequacy or ill effects of existing means-tested programs. By analyzing articles on such a broad array of issue areas, I ensure the generalizability of the findings presented here.

Coding Procedures

Article coding was done in two stages.[4] The initial stage identified the policy-focused and problem-focused articles in each of the three policy areas. Policy-focused articles are those that center on policy making in Congress or on federal legislation that is being drafted, has been proposed, or has recently passed. Problem-focused articles center on issues that are of broad societal concern. If an article gives equal weight to the discussion of a societal problem and to the discussion of legislation designed to ameliorate that problem, both codes were applied. Articles primarily centered on other topics—such as campaign platforms, local policy initiatives, or scientific innovations—are not considered either "problem" or "policy" focused. Such articles were not eligible for further codes.

In a second round of coding, I examined the content of the policy-and problem-focused articles in detail. This included the assignment of codes identifying the presence of the conflict frame, the economic frame, and the human-interest frame. Codes indicating the presence of substantive information about the content of a bill or the severity of a societal problem were also developed and applied. All of these codes are described in detail below.

The Conflict Frame

The literature on conflict-focused news reporting identifies several sensational elements of the political process that journalists often highlight to attract readers and viewers. My coding of the conflict frame was informed by this literature, drawing particularly on Newman et al.'s (1992) description of the conflict frame, Jamieson (1992) and Patterson's (1993) descriptions of "strategy coverage," Cappella and Jamieson's (1996) typology of news coverage, Jacobs and Shapiro's (2000) discussion of the "strategy and conflict frame," and Hibbing and Theiss-Morse's (2002) discussion of public response to the policy-making process. Using these sources as references, I developed five codes that capture distinct elements of the conflict frame: polarized forces, heated conflict, substantive debate, parliamentary tactics, and political calculus.

As described by Newman et al. (1992), the generic conflict frame focuses on "polarized forces—'the two sides of the issue'" (64). Therefore, to receive the polarized forces code, the article must be focused around two groups that are competing or at odds over an issue or piece of legislation. The headline and opening sentences of an article are critical to the assignment of this code. If the article described a dispute between two actors or groups within the first four sentences, setting the article up as an examination of the "two sides of the issue," the article received the "polarized forces" code. For example, each of the lead paragraphs below received the polarized forces code:

> When President Obama squared off with House Republicans in a question-and-answer session on Friday, perhaps no issue was more contentious than health care. Among Mr. Obama's boldest assertions was that Democrats had put forward a mostly centrist plan and that Republicans attacked it as "some Bolshevik plot" (Herszenhorn 2010)

> President Bush and the Democratic-controlled Congress prepared Monday for a showdown over the future of health insurance for more than 10 million children (Pear and Hulse 2007).

> Opening a rift within the religious right, a House Republican today introduced a constitutional amendment that would provide for prayer in public schools, a proposal that some other conservatives and religious groups say goes in the wrong direction (Seelye 1995).

The heated conflict code goes one step beyond "polarized forces," identifying debates between elites that have become uncivil. It is applied to articles in which the author repeatedly characterizes the interactions between elites or the debate itself as heated or akin to war. For instance, articles that contain at least two instances where a disagreement is described as a "fight," or "attack" would receive this code. In the examples below, words like "wrath," "battle," and "exploded" are used to characterize tensions between lawmakers:

By proposing sharp slashes in Federal aid to education, President Reagan has run head on into the collective wrath of what former Representative Edith Green once called "the educational-industrial complex" (Hunter 1981).

Armed with conflicting economic studies, they waged verbal battle over job losses, inflationary effects and the question of whether Democrats or Republicans were the truer champions of workers at the lowest end of the scale (Rasky 1989).

The perennial tension between governors and mayors exploded again last week in their responses to President Bush's proposal to turn over $15 billion of Federal programs to the states (Pear 1991).

Substantive debate comprises an additional element of the conflict frame. Many members of the public prefer to see elites in agreement about the best course of action for the country and dislike disagreement between elites (Hibbing and Theiss Morse 2002). For that reason, I track the occurrence of substantive debate. In the context of a societal problem, the code is applied to articles that include a two-sided discussion of the causes or severity of social ills like poverty, drug addiction, or failing schools. In the context of public policy, the code is applied to articles that contain a two-sided discussion of the efficacy, merits, or potential effects of a given piece of legislation. The two excerpts below provide examples of substantive debate, first in the context of a societal problem and then in the context of policy making:

Substantive Debate in a Problem-Focused Article:
A new nationwide survey finds startling numbers of students in the 6th to 12th grades who say they have shot at someone or have been shot at themselves. The survey of 2,508 students in 96 schools across the country by the pollster Louis Harris, painted a bleak portrait of violence and fear among American schoolchildren. Several experts on guns were skeptical about the results, saying the figures were higher than those in any previous surveys. They suggested either that the students might be exaggerating or that the sample might have been skewed (Chira 1993).

Substantive Debate in a Policy-Focused Article:
House Republicans said today that they wanted to cut $16.5 billion from the food stamp program over the next five years by establishing strict new

work requirements for recipients and by trimming the growth in benefits. The proposal represents a fundamental shift in the design of the program, which serves as the ultimate safety net for more than 27 million poor Americans. Democrats say the overall bill is cruel to women and children because it would, for example, scrap the national school lunch program and give the money to the states as well as bar the use of Federal money to provide cash assistance to unmarried teen-agers (Pear 1995).

In addition to the three codes described above, which could potentially apply to both problem- and policy-focused articles, the final two conflict codes are specific to articles that focus on lawmaking.[5] One important aspect of the conflict frame is the emphasis on the strategies employed by opposing actors (Jacobs and Shapiro 2000). This information is part of a narrative that treats politics like a game by examining who is "winning" and "losing" in Washington (Cappella and Jamieson 1997; Patterson 1993). I, therefore, apply two codes that identify elements of this strategy-focused, horse race coverage. Each emphasizes the tactics employed by opposing "teams." The first, "parliamentary tactics," is applied to articles that detail the strategies used by lawmakers within the legislative arena to advance their preferred policies and to defeat the policies they oppose. This includes discussions of delay tactics and the strategic timing of votes, tactics used to limit debate, filibustering, presidential veto threats, methods of ensuring party loyalty, the strategic addition of amendments, party-line votes, and disputes over committee jurisdiction.

The second code, "political calculus," is applied to articles that discuss the political consequences that could result from a bill's passage or defeat. This includes discussions of the electoral importance of a piece of legislation for a particular candidate or party, discussions of the impact of a bill's passage or defeat on presidential job approval numbers, etc. Discussions of the political strategies used to rally popular support for a piece of legislation also fall under the purview of this code. Examples of both codes are provided below:

Parliamentary Tactics:
President Bush has threatened to veto the House bill, developed entirely by Democrats, and a more modest bipartisan measure, expected to win Senate approval this week. Republicans tried to block consideration of the House bill and complained that it was being rammed through the House without any opportunity for amendment (Pear 2007).

Political Calculus:

[The president] showed that he was perfectly willing to play political hard-
ball in pursuit of his agenda. Using tactics reminiscent of President Bill Clinton's 'permanent campaign,' he took to the road to sell the tax cut in campaign style trips to states of Senate Democrats who may be vulnerable in
2002. The Republican National Committee used automated calls to pressure
some Democrats, and the White House's conservative allies took to the airwaves (Mitchell 2001).

Together, these two codes represent the facets of the conflict frame
that are related entirely to the legislative process, as opposed to the substance of the legislation under consideration.

Alternative Frames: Economic, Human Interest, and Substance Focus

In addition to the conflict frame, I also track the use of the economic
frame and the human-interest frame. The economic frame is likely to
convey important substantive information because of its focus on the
cost and economic impact of policies and societal problems. Such information might focus public attention on the relationship between a policy
and the size of the government or the national deficit. Similarly, its use
might help to quantify the severity of a societal problem. By highlighting
these substantive details, articles that employ the economic frame may
heighten the salience of such considerations.

I developed five codes to measure the degree to which articles employed an economic frame. The first indicates the presence of spending
or deficit estimates related to a societal problem or policy change. The
second identifies references to anticipated changes in macroeconomic
indicators (such as the unemployment rate or inflation) that could result
or have resulted from a given policy or societal problem. The third code
identifies descriptions of proposed tax increases, and a fourth code identifies descriptions of proposed tax cuts or credits. The last code is an
indicator of the prominence of the spending and economic information
found in the article. If the economic information is provided in the headline or first four sentences of the article—establishing the centrality of
that information—the article is given the "economic lead" code.

The human-interest frame "focuses on describing individuals and groups who are likely to be affected by an issue" (Newman et al. 1992, 69). Such articles "put a human face" on a policy or "paint a portrait" of a problem through example. Articles that include such a description in the first four sentences are given the code "human interest lead." Articles that include such descriptions in the body of the article are given the code "human interest focus."

The last code, "substance focus," identifies articles that are primarily informative in nature, meaning they provide facts and figures (that are not in dispute) about a policy or problem. For policy-focused articles, a substance focus means that at least 50% of the article is devoted to explaining or describing a bill's substantive provisions (which may include cost estimates). For problem-focused articles, a substance focus means that at least 50% of the article is devoted to discussing the causes, reach, or severity of a societal problem. Articles that receive this code typically quote recent studies or reports and offer statistics related to the problem or policy. Human-interest stories that paint a portrait of the struggles faced by one family or one community, but do not provide facts about the degree to which the example is indicative of a larger problem, do not receive the "substance focus" code.

Using the coding scheme outlined here, I explore the degree to which problem- and policy-focused news reports respectively use the conflict frame, the economic frame, and the human-interest frame.

Conflict in the News

To assess the prevalence of the conflict frame in articles about policy making as compared with articles about societal problems, table 2.2 displays the share of each that was given one of the five conflict codes. This information is provided separately for each issue area. Notice that for all three issue areas, the conflict codes are more prevalent among the policy-focused articles than among the problem-focused ones. For instance, 76% of the health policy articles received at least one conflict code and 53% received two or more conflict codes. In contrast, only 27% of the health problem articles received at least one conflict code, and only 10% received two or more conflict codes. The same pattern is seen in the education dataset, where 71% of the policy-focused articles received at least one conflict code as compared with just 20% of the problem-focused articles. Even in the welfare dataset, which had the lowest overall percent-

TABLE 2.2. **Application of Conflict Codes, across Issue Areas and Article Type.**

	Policy-Focused Articles		Problem-Focused Articles	
Code	Number	Percentage	Number	Percentage
Health	182	100%	102	100%
Policy- *and* Problem-Focused	3	4%	3	2%
At Least One Conflict Code	**138**	**76%**	**28**	**27%**
Two or More Conflict Codes	**97**	**53%**	**10**	**10%**
Polarized Forces	52	29%	3	3%
Heated Conflict	60	33%	8	8%
Substantive Debate	72	40%	27	27%
Parliamentary Tactics	71	39%	0	0%
Political Calculus	49	27%	0	0%
Education	76	100%	148	100%
Policy- *and* Problem-Focused	3	4%	3	2%
At Least One Conflict Code	**54**	**71%**	**30**	**20%**
Two or More Conflict Codes	**35**	**46%**	**12**	**8%**
Polarized Forces	29	38%	10	7%
Heated Conflict	24	32%	8	5%
Substantive Debate	24	32%	26	18%
Parliamentary Tactics	11	14%	0	0%
Political Calculus	15	20%	1	1%
Welfare	168	100%	155	100%
Policy- *and* Problem-Focused	11	7%	11	7%
At Least One Conflict Code	**108**	**64%**	**21**	**14%**
Two or More Conflict Codes	**78**	**46%**	**5**	**3%**
Polarized Forces	79	47%	6	4%
Heated Conflict	46	27%	3	2%
Substantive Debate	45	27%	11	7%
Parliamentary Tactics	39	23%	0	0%
Political Calculus	29	17%	6	4%

age of articles with a conflict code, conflict was still found in most policy-focused articles (64%) and was roughly 4.5 times less likely among the problem-focused articles.

Not only was conflict more prevalent, overall, in the policy-focused articles, but conflict was also more likely to appear in the headline or opening sentences of these reports. More than one third of all the policy-focused articles (37.5%) were structured as a debate between "polarized forces"—opening with a description of the two sides of the fight. Further, in roughly 30% of the policy-focused articles, the conflict was described as heated or uncivil with language such as "poisonous partisan debate" (Pear and Toner 2004), "surly clashes between the parties" (Hulse 2003), and "partisan brawl" (Pear 2010). In contrast, very few problem-focused articles opened with descriptions of two opposing actors. The "polar-

ized forces" code was applied to just 7% of the education problem articles, 4% of the welfare problem articles, and 3% of the health problem
articles.

Three examples help to illustrate the tone established in policy-
focused articles that opened with descriptions of "polarized forces."

Example A:
Headline: *The Nation*: The Minimum-Wage Fight Isn't Really about Pay

In a Congressional session thus far devoid of serious policymaking, it is probably fitting that the first showdown between Democrats and President Bush
comes over the largely symbolic question of how much to raise the minimum
wage (Rasky 1989).

Example B:
Headline: Clinton Raises Stakes in the Battle over a Bigger Medicare Pot

President Clinton escalated the fight over Medicare spending today, demand-
ing that Congress shift money to health programs for poor people, disabled
children and legal immigrants.

But Republicans rebuffed White House pleas to negotiate on the issue and
said they felt they had the upper hand (Pear 2000).

Example C:
Headline: Congressional Memo; Fate of Tax Credits Rests with Houses
Divided

Representative Bill Thomas of California, who can accelerate from disagreement to outright scorn faster than anyone on Capitol Hill, had a characteristi-
cally withering remark this week for a provision he disliked in a Senate tax bill.

"Sounds like a Senate product," said Mr. Thomas, a Republican and chairman of the Ways and Means Committee, not bothering to conceal his contempt for legislation sent his way by the upper house (Firestone 2003).

In the headlines above, the words "fight," "battle," and "divided" are
respectively used to establish that two groups are at odds with one another. In examples A and C, the lead paragraphs go on to further char-

acterize the conflict—with words like "showdown," "scorn," and "contempt"—without providing information about the substance of the debate. In fact, example A describes the legislation itself as "symbolic." Example B is the only one of the three to characterize the conflict and to offer a description of the substantive disagreement between lawmakers within the first few sentences.

The tone, content, and structure of these examples are representative of the numerous policy-focused reports that received the "polarized forces" code. By describing the battle between actors in the headline and lead paragraph, these articles established the primacy of information about the acrimonious lawmaking process. When substantive information about the policy was given, it was provided within the context of this conflict. For instance, government spending and deficit estimates were frequently provided in policy-focused articles (see table 2.3). Forty-six percent of welfare policy-focused articles contained such estimates, 38% of education policy-focused articles contained them, and 24% of health policy-focused articles contained spending or deficit projections. These figures were not typically the focus of the articles that contained them, however. Spending and deficit estimates were prominently placed (in the first four sentences) in approximately 25% of the welfare-focused articles, 14% of the health policy articles, and just 9% of the education policy articles. More often, these figures were located in the body of the article and were, themselves, presented as topics of debate among lawmakers. Opponents of a given policy often argued that it would cost more than proponents estimated, that it would not be deficit neutral, or that it would not save as much money as expected. For example, an article published on November 11, 2009, outlined the contradictory claims made by lawmakers about the cost of "Obamacare":

> Over two days of debate on the Senate floor about the motion to move ahead with the major health care legislation, Democrats and Republicans fired volley after volley of contradictory claims about the proposed bill . . . Lindsey Graham, Republican of South Carolina: "The bill we are moving to consider will cost $2.5 trillion once fully implemented; nearly three times the official C.B.O. score of $848 billion. The Democrats are playing a shell game to hide the true cost of this legislation." Judd Gregg, Republican of New Hampshire: "When all this new spending occurs, this bill will cost $2.5 trillion over that 10-year period—$2.5 trillion. That is the real cost of this bill." Robert Menen-

TABLE 2.3. **Spending and Economic Codes, across Issue Areas and Article Type.**

Code	Policy-Focused Articles		Problem-Focused Articles	
	Number	Percentage	Number	Percentage
Health	182	100%	102	100%
Economic Lead	25	14%	13	13%
Macroeconomic Implications	9	5%	3	3%
Spending or Deficit Estimates	50	27%	11	11%
Tax Increases Described	19	10%	0	0%
Tax Cuts Described	10	5%	1	1%
Education	76	100%	148	100%
Economic Lead	7	9%	1	1%
Macroeconomic Implications	0	0%	0	0%
Spending or Deficit Estimates	29	38%	6	4%
Tax Increases Described	0	0%	0	0%
Tax Cuts Described	0	0%	0	0%
Welfare	168	100%	155	100%
Economic Lead	42	25%	10	6%
Macroeconomic Implications	4	2%	11	7%
Spending or Deficit Estimates	77	46%	28	18%
Tax Increases Described	5	3%	0	0%
Tax Cuts Described	20	12%	0	0%

dez, Democrat of New Jersey: "This bill actually cuts the deficit by $130 billion in the first 10 years and $650 billion in the second 10 years" (Herszenhorn 2009).

Of all the policy-focused articles that contained spending and deficit estimates, 92% also received at least one conflict code, and 61% received two or more conflict codes. Put differently, information about government spending was rarely provided in a "just the facts" sort of way. Rather, this information was woven into the overarching theme of conflict between elites, as was much of the substantive information about the content of legislation. In addition to cost, the merits, efficacy, and likely consequences of particular provisions were frequent topics of debate. Across the three issue areas, substantive debate was seen in 40% of the health policy articles, 32% of the education policy articles, and 27% of the welfare policy articles. However, less than one third of the policy-focused articles devoted ample space to factual—conflict-free—descriptions of the bill's substantive provisions.

Information about the legislative and political tactics employed by those on either side of the debate also contributed to the conflict story-line (see table 2.2).[6] Overall, approximately 50% of the policy-focused articles received one of the two "tactics" codes. Such coverage was most prevalent among the health policy articles—39% contained descriptions of parliamentary tactics and 27% included descriptions of political calculus. Descriptions of parliamentary and political tactics were least common among education policy articles—14% included parliamentary tactics and 20% included political calculus.

An examination of these descriptions helps to clarify why many Americans have a negative perception of policy debate. As illustrated by the examples below, discussions of the parliamentary and political tactics employed by lawmakers focus public attention on opposing party leaders, what each has to gain or lose from a bill's passage, and which has the upper hand.

Parliamentary Tactics:

Democrats were narrowly defeated today on another important amendment to the Republicans' welfare bill. Their amendment, rejected by a vote of 50 to 49, sought to prevent states from slashing their contributions to basic welfare programs. But the Republicans prevailed only after their leaders made new concessions on the issue to hold their party's moderates (Toner 1995).

Congress broke for Thanksgiving with a final burst of partisan recrimina-tions over the conduct of a session that produced Medicare changes, tax cuts and hard feelings certain to spill over into the 2004 campaign. . . . Democrats asserted that Republicans, in their drive to prove they could deliver when controlling both the House and the Senate, badly bent Congressional rules and resorted to "brass knuckles" to force through flawed legislation that will backfire with the public (Hulse 2003).

Political Calculus:

The same political concerns that compelled President Bush to announce a "comprehensive health reform program" today also obliged him to be vague about many details. . . . While it has become politically necessary for candi-dates to address health care in general, it is virtually impossible for them to make specific proposals without offending somebody. Thus Dr. Louis W. Sul-livan, the Secretary of Health and Human Services, and White House offi-cials were unable to answer important questions today about how the Presi-dent's plan would work (Pear 1992).

Mr. Bush's budget began an ideologically charged debate in a midterm election year, with his party's control of Congress at stake. . . . The Democratic Senatorial Campaign Committee quickly dispatched talking points tailored to hot Senate races. "White House budget forces Santorum to choose between Pennsylvania and Bush," said one set of talking points focused on Senator Rick Santorum of Pennsylvania, a Republican facing a difficult re-election fight (Toner 2006).

In these examples, debate is not presented as an effort to develop the best policy for the American people; it is presented as a "battle" between the parties, each of whom has a vested interest in being the victor. Such coverage contributes to the widely held view that policy debate serves the interests of politicians rather than the interests of the public.

Lawmakers and journalists are both aware of the role this framing plays in shaping public discourse on policy. Jacobs and Shapiro (2000) note that lawmakers promoting policy reforms craft positive messages in an effort to "override the press's preoccupation with the maneuvering of politicians" (49). Lawmakers understand that press coverage focused on the "motivations, intentions, and strategic behavior of officeholders" can serve the interests of the reform's opponents by helping to generate public uncertainty about the reform (Jacobs and Shapiro 2000, 60).

Journalists, who occasionally reflect on their own practices in print, also recognize the impact this type of coverage can have. For instance, in August of 1994, as it became clear that President Clinton would be unable to pass his health reform legislation, the *New York Times* ran an article with the headline: "Making Sausage: The Art of Reprocessing the Democratic Process" (Toner 1994). In the article, the author described how lawmakers and the news media both slipped into "campaign mode" during the long fight over health reform and "focused on whether Mr. Clinton was winning or losing" rather than the substance of the debate (Toner 1994). This focus frustrated members of the public—who purportedly wanted more substantive information—and perpetuated partisanship in Washington. The article goes on to state, "In short, there is substantial evidence that the deadlock on health care is a monument not to the Framers' system, but to what we have done to it: a harrowing example of what happens when the tools, techniques and philosophy of the modern campaign are brought to bear on the policy-making process" (Toner 1994).

The press covered the debate over health care reform in 2009 and

2010 similarly. The contentious reform plan ignited fierce debate on Capitol Hill and that debate was amplified by members of the press, who fixated on the strategies employed by members of Congress and the White House. As detailed in chapter 5, the public's response to the debate and the media's coverage of it was largely negative. An excerpt from an article published by the *New York Times* in early 2010 helps to illustrate why. One of the interviews included in the article reveals that Americans were fed up with partisanship and felt lawmakers had lost sight of the underlying problems that needed to be fixed:

> Donny Seyfer, the manager of an auto repair shop here, had high hopes when President Obama and Congress tackled health care as their top priority early last year. "This is good," Mr. Seyfer remembers thinking. He expected Congress to "find out what Americans wanted." But, he said in an interview at his shop, the Congressional debate deteriorated into a partisan brawl, and Congress has virtually ignored his biggest concern: holding down health costs.
>
> "I am an automotive diagnostician," Mr. Seyfer said. "We look for the root cause of problems. If we treat the symptoms, the problem always comes back. With health care, we are not treating the root cause: Why does it cost so much?" (Pear 2010).

Journalists' focus on the political conflict left many Americans with the sense that everyone in Washington had lost sight of the needs of ordinary people. The lack of focus on the plan's substance meant few had a firm understanding of how the various reform proposals would fix problems and impact their lives. And, indeed, just as I hypothesized, very few articles both outlined problems in the health care system and described how the reform proposals would redress them. Table 2.2 shows the percentage of stories that received both the "policy" and "problem" codes. Note that in all three issue areas, societal problems and policy solutions were almost always discussed separately. The number of articles that gave equal weight to societal problems and proposed governmental solutions is just eight in the case of health, three in the case of education, and eleven in the case of welfare. More often, policy-focused reports gave only a cursory description of the problem that prompted the introduction of legislation in Congress. Likewise, it was not uncommon for problem-focused articles to make no mention whatsoever of proposed policy solutions. This pattern of news coverage contributes to the sentiment expressed by Mr. Seyfer that lawmakers are "not treating the root cause" of societal problems.

The Content of Problem-Focused Articles

When societal problems were at the center of news reports, the frames employed by journalists were distinct from those used in conjunction with policy-focused reports. Not only were problem-focused articles less likely to be structured around the "two sides" of an issue, as shown in table 2.4, they were also more apt to focus on facts. Roughly two-thirds of all the problem-focused articles received the "substance focus" code. The majority of the problem-focused articles, thus, spent ample time describing the given problem, often using statistics to quantify its size and growth over time. And unlike with conflict-focused reports, these statistics were not typically up for debate. Because the substantive information given in the problem-focused articles was provided as fact rather than as a topic of dispute, conflict was not prominent in these articles. Two examples illustrate this point:

The well-being of children in America has declined dramatically since 1970, according to an index that measures aspects of "social health" like infant mortality and drug abuse. Particularly devastating to the nation's youth

TABLE 2.4. **Substance Focus and Human Interest Codes, across Issue Areas and Article Type.**

Code	Policy-Focused Articles		Problem-Focused Articles	
	Number	Percentage	Number	Percentage
Health	182	100%	102	100%
Substance Focus	43	24%	69	68%
Human-Interest Focus	0	0%	17	17%
Human-Interest Lead	3	2%	20	20%
Education	76	100%	148	100%
Substance Focus	31	41%	100	68%
Human-Interest Focus	0	0%	25	6%
Human-Interest Lead	0	0%	39	26%
Welfare	168	100%	155	100%
Substance Focus	64	38%	92	60%
Human-Interest Focus	3	2%	48	31%
Human-Interest Lead	3	2%	45	29%

have been sharp increases in the numbers of children and teen-agers who are abused, who live in poverty and who commit suicide, the index found (Goleman 1989).

About one in four classes at public middle schools and high schools is taught by a teacher not trained in the subject, and the problem is much worse in schools that serve poor and minority students, according to a report released today by the Education Trust (AP 2002).

As illustrated here, reports about societal problems that were substance-focused typically presented information in a dry, straightforward manner. Seldom were characterizations of the problems disputed.

When problem-focused articles were embellished to add interest, it was most often through the application of the human-interest frame (see table 2.4). Twenty percent of the health problem articles opened with a description of an individual or community that had been affected by an issue like loss of health coverage or chronic illness. Twenty-six percent of the education problem articles employed a human-interest lead, and 29% of the welfare problem articles did so. No more than 2% of the policy-focused articles employed a human-interest lead in any of the three issue areas.

The human interest-frame establishes a tone that stands in contrast to the combative tone of the conflict frame. Compare the following human-interest leads with the "polarized forces" leads provided above:

The boy seemed a loose tangle of arms and legs as he spoke of spending many of his school days last year at home watching cartoons or outside riding his bicycle. Whenever he rode, graffiti and urban decay whisked by as he pedaled along in his New York City neighborhood, flattening spent crack vials with as little alarm as if they were fallen leaves (Marriott 1990).

As she weighs bunches of purple grapes or rings up fat chicken legs at the supermarket where she works, Fannie Payne cannot keep from daydreaming. "It's difficult to work at a grocery store all day, looking at all the food I can't buy," Mrs. Payne said. "So I imagine filling up my cart with one of those big orders and bringing home enough food for all my kids" (Becker 2001).

SHALIA WATTS, a government employee from Sacramento, received some upsetting news in June: the health maintenance organization to which she belongs, Health Net, will no longer be available through her employer next year. At the same time, she said, she found that the monthly premium for the Blue Shield H.M.O. she chose as a replacement would be $110, almost double what she pays now (Kobliner 2002).

These introductions paint sympathetic portraits of individual struggles. They invite the reader to consider what it would be like to stand in the shoes of another person, and suggest that the issue he or she is facing is a matter of public concern.

This framing seems natural because we have seen descriptions of societal problems discussed this way time and again. However, the human-interest frame is just one of many frames that could be applied to discussions of hunger, crumbling schools, nursing shortages, and so on. In particular, articles that discuss societal problems could be framed in terms of conflict by providing two-sided discussions of the causes and severity of social ills. They could, likewise, include discussions of who is to blame for these problems and disputes over who ought to bear responsibility for fixing them. In fact, some problem-focused articles do include just these types of discussions. But far more often, debate and conflict are not part of the dialogue about societal problems until the discussion enters the arena of government action. Until that time, agreement that the problem is bad and should be corrected dominates the public discourse, as it does in the examples above. The lack of conflict in problem-focused news coverage helps to explain why many Americans believe "'most' people agree on the most important problem facing the country," and think finding the solution to it should be as straightforward as identifying the problem (Hibbing and Theiss-Morse 2002, 145).

Conclusion

I have demonstrated that the information the news media provide about the substance of new laws is packaged in predictable ways. Many policy-focused news reports are structured around "polarized forces" and high-light points of disagreement between political elites. These debates are often characterized as heated or uncivil and detail the parliamentary and political tactics used to wage legislative battle. The substantive information provided to news consumers is given within the context of this fight. Information about the problems reform proposals seek to ameliorate are typically discussed in separate articles using alternative frames. In this way, societal problems and policy solutions are uncoupled in public discourse.

These findings help to explain Americans' negative perceptions of policy debate. Because news reports do not focus on the link between policy proposals and the problems they are designed to redress, conflict over public policy does not seem aimed at problem solving. Instead, debate seems to be a tool lawmakers use to advance their own political careers—leaving many Americans with the impression that the policy-making process is corrupt, dysfunctional, and ridiculous. In fact, these are the very words that Americans used to describe Congressional debate during two periods of heightened conflict—the period leading up to the passage of the Affordable Care Act and the period of budget negotiations in 2011 (Pew 2010c; Pew 2011). I now turn to how the public responds to the policies they associate with a broken lawmaking process.

CHAPTER THREE

Love the Substance, Hate the Plan

Now, I recognize that people watching tonight have differing views about taxes and debt, energy and health care. But no matter what party they belong to, I bet most Americans are thinking the same thing right about now: Nothing will get done in Washington this year, or next year, or maybe even the year after that, because **Washington is broken**.

We need to end the notion that the two parties must be locked in a perpetual campaign of mutual destruction; that politics is about clinging to rigid ideologies instead of building consensus around common-sense ideas. —Remarks by the President in State of the Union Address, 2012 (emphasis added)

President Obama's first term saw the passage of two pieces of legislation that are sure to go down in history as landmarks: The American Recovery and Reinvestment Act of 2009 and The Patient Protection and Affordable Care Act of 2010. While the former pumped roughly $800 billion into the faltering economy, the latter reformed the health insurance industry and mandated universal coverage. The Dodd-Frank Act, the Lilly Ledbetter Fair Pay Act, and the repeal of Don't Ask, Don't Tell are among the dozens of other important laws also signed during President Obama's first term.

Given these accomplishments, the headlines could have read: "Another important bill signed into law." Or: "Lawmakers work tirelessly on behalf of constituents." But they did not. Instead, as outlined in the last chapter, they described partisan arguing and a dysfunctional political system.

Journalists make choices about how to cover lawmaking based on the norms of their profession and the need to attract readers, viewers, and advertisers. Focusing on the horse race, the partisan conflicts, and the strategies employed by lawmakers helps them accomplish these goals. But just as President Obama stated in his 2012 State of the Union

Address, this campaign mentality (among both journalists and politicians) leads many Americans to believe the government is broken.

The use of the conflict frame amplifies the partisan rhetoric in Washington by presenting political elites as "polarized forces" (Jacobs and Shapiro 2000; Newman et al. 1992; Montpetit 2016). Viewed through this lens, the actions of politicians seem petty and self-interested. The legitimacy of differences of opinion over the best course of action for the country is lost in the cacophony of partisan quarreling trumpeted by the press. The news media seldom highlight lawmakers' efforts at compromise or their dedication to constituent's needs. Little attention is given to the underlying problems at issue, their causes, and the needs of the groups most affected. And the details of the bills generating such debate are also frequently subordinated to descriptions of the partisan conflict. Simply put, the conflict frame highlights the aspects of lawmaking that many Americans view as a sign of a broken government. By obscuring the problem solving aspects of lawmaking, the frame gives the impression that no one in Washington is trying to "build consensus around common-sense ideas" (Remarks by the President, 2012).

When thinking about a piece of legislation, people do not separate or compartmentalize this type of information about the lawmaking process from substantive information about a program's cost and provisions. Instead, all the information people learn about a bill becomes linked up with it in their minds. The more the news media focus on debate and discord among lawmakers, the more salient that information becomes for average Americans. Because of its heightened salience, non-substantive information about the broken lawmaking process can overwhelm the influence of substantive considerations in the formation of policy opinions. Here, I use two experiments to demonstrate the negative effect of political conflict on support for policies associated with it.

How the Conflict Frame Shapes Public Opinion

Recall that exposure to heated debate is expected to influence policy opinions both directly and indirectly. The direct process by which conceptions of the lawmaking process influence policy attitudes is straightforward. When individuals associate a particular policy with controversy and debate, those considerations become part of the mix of information that is aggregated in forming an attitude toward the policy. For individuals who hold a negative view of debate—those who view debate as a sign that lawmakers are pursuing their own political interests—attitudes toward the policy itself will sour from this negative association. The more the news media focus on partisan squabbles in Washington, the stronger the association will be and the more heavily these negative conceptions of the lawmaking process will weigh in to the individual's overall assessment of the policy.

This direct effect is most likely among individuals who do not have strong policy opinions or a lot of knowledge about lawmaking (whom we might call political novices). These individuals want lawmakers to fix the problem of the day but do not have a strong affinity for a particular policy solution. Instead, they believe there is a "best" solution that conscientious lawmakers would select without debate if they had the public interest at heart (Hibbing and Theiss-Morse 2002). This represents a fundamental misunderstanding of how the policy-making process works. A best solution to a complex problem like smog, crime, unemployment, or homelessness is rarely self-evident. Debate can be a useful tool for lawmakers who must attempt to predict the future benefits and costs of competing proposals. But because they do not recognize this legitimate role of debate, individuals with low levels of knowledge about lawmaking are more likely to view debate as a sign of a dysfunctional government than are those who know more (Hibbing and Theiss-Morse 2002). All debate seems politically motivated to these novices, and this belief is only strengthened by the media's portrayal of it.

The conflict frame highlights disagreements between the parties and emphasizes the political repercussions of the issue for those on either side of the fight. As I demonstrated in chapter 2, this pattern of news coverage suggests that policy debate is a fundamentally political process rather than an exercise in problem solving. News reports rarely focus on the link between policy proposals and the problems they are designed to redress. Because the conflict frame highlights the role of legislation in a larger partisan conflict and obscures its potential for problem solving, news reports that employ it strengthen the belief that heavily debated proposals are designed to advance political goals rather than the public interest.

The more people hear about conflict, strategy, and the horse race, the more salient and accessible this information becomes their minds. Because the political novice does not hold strong, stable policy preferences, she will be particularly dependent upon the mix of information that is salient to her when she is asked to give an opinion about the policy. In the words of Zaller and Feldman (1992), she will use the information "at the top of the head" to form an opinion. This information is very likely to be a mix of negative considerations about the political battle in Washington because of the media's routine use of the conflict frame. As a result, she is likely to express disapproval of the proposal.

Policy debate sends a different signal to political sophisticates—those with stronger policy preferences and a better understanding of how the lawmaking process works. These individuals want to see policies adopted that are as close as possible to their own ideological preferences. This means they watch debates unfolding on the Hill looking for clues that can help them determine just how liberal or conservative the bills under consideration are. When a proposed law ignites fierce debate between the parties, these sophisticates view the conflict as a sign that the proposal is ideologically extreme. They assume that the parties could find room to compromise over moderate proposals and that debate means the proposal is either so liberal or so conservative (depending on which party introduced the bill) that the parties are unable to find common ground. Political sophisticates, therefore, believe debate is motivated by ideological disagreement.

Political sophisticates can decide how much they like or dislike the bill in this way, by figuring out how closely it aligns with their own policy preferences. Some individuals will prefer more ideologically extreme bills because they, themselves, have extreme preferences. But most Americans will be turned off by ideological extremism because most Americans hold moderate views. In the aggregate, it is this penchant for moderation that underscores the well-known "thermostatic response" (Wlezien 1995). When citizens see their government enacting policies that are too liberal, the public responds by calling for more conservative legislation and vice versa. In this way, public opinion reins in ideological extremism at the macro level (Erikson, MacKuen, and Stimson 2002). At the individual level, citizens should similarly reject policy proposals that they believe are far from their own ideological preferences. The presence or absence of partisan debate can, therefore, influence public policy attitudes indirectly by altering the perceived distance between the individual and the bill on the left/right ideological spectrum. The further the individual believes the bill is from himself or herself, the less likely the individual is to support the bill.

Whether the effect is direct or indirect, most Americans will be more critical of policies associated with heated debate than they will be of policies not associated with such debate—even if they like the specific provisions that comprise the legislation. Using an experimental design, I test this hypothesis. I also examine the impact of exposure to debate on the belief that the policy-making process is broken, and on citizen's assessments of the bill's ideology. Lastly, I examine differences in the policy views of political sophisticates and political novices.

Study Participants

The experiment was first conducted using a student sample at a large public university and then replicated (with minor alterations) as part of the 2012 Cooperative Congressional Election Study (CCES).[1] The results of both administrations of the experiment are reported here because each has particular strengths and weaknesses. The adult sample provided by the CCES is more representative of the general population than is the student sample. For instance, CCES participants range in age from eighteen to eighty-seven, with the average age being fifty-three. Nearly 28% of the sample had never attended college. These demographic characteristics stand in contrast to the student sample, for which the mean age is nineteen, and, of course, all respondents have had college courses. However, the CCES sample was collected within the context of a national election campaign. As Patterson (1993) and others have demonstrated, campaign coverage is particularly centered on the horse race—meaning public affairs reports during this period will be especially focused on the aspects of political debate that this study seeks to investigate. As a result, the CCES respondents may have been saturated with exposure to political conflict before receiving the experimental treatments.

In contrast, the student data were collected during the fall of 2011, outside the context of a national election. This makes the timing of the student study preferable to the CCES study. The use of student data also presents a hard test of my hypothesis. The policy described in the experimental treatments proposes to increase funding for public education. Students are particularly apt to favor education funding, giving them a reason to support the policy even when it is associated with conflict. In these ways, the two samples complement each other and provide strong evidence when taken together. I discuss each in turn below.

Experimental Design: The Student Sample

Participants in the student study were first asked to complete a questionnaire that gathered demographic information as well as information on party identification, political ideology, political knowledge, and interest in politics. Participants were then randomly assigned to one of six treatment groups and asked to read a short vignette (approximately 250 words long) about an education policy. Education was chosen because it was not a topic of national debate while the experiment was in the field, thereby minimizing the influence of real world policy debate on the experimental findings.

The results of the content analysis detailed in chapter 2 were used to inform the content of the vignettes, which were modeled after real *New York Times* articles about the Obama health care plan (where education was substituted for health care).[2] As many verbatim statements from the real articles were used as possible. The vignettes were also designed by a graphic artist to look like articles downloaded from the *New York Times*. However, while the real articles attribute quotes to named party leaders (like Nancy Pelosi), no actual members of Congress were referenced by name in the treatments. The treatments reference speakers with titles, such as "Committee Chairman," or use made-up names. This was done to prevent attitudes toward specific political figures from influencing participant responses.

All of the treatments open with a lead paragraph that describes the education bill as one "designed to reform K through 12 education by providing vastly more resources for schools and teachers." The six treatments—summarized in table 3.1—differ in that they vary both the way the debate is framed (emphasizing either heated or civil debate) and the substance of the debate. The "heated" treatments, which highlight partisan conflict, use the headline, "Partisan Battle on Education Heats Up." The articles themselves describe the bill as "hotly contested," note that "the debate has deteriorated into a partisan brawl," and state that "Democrats will have to close ranks and vote as a bloc to pass the bill without Republican support." All of the treatments that employ a civil debate frame describe the bill as a bipartisan one, note that the bill is gaining momentum in the Senate, and state that lawmakers are working "to find common ground."

The three different substantive treatments each focus on a distinct facet of real world policy debate, as reported by the news media. Those

TABLE 3.1. **Description of Experimental Treatments.**

	Tactics	Spending	Efficacy
Heated Debate Frame	Frame: "Partisan brawl," "hotly contested bill"	Frame: "Partisan brawl," "hotly contested bill"	Frame: "Partisan brawl," "hotly contested bill"
	Substance: Bundle of amendments attached to bill	Substance: Disagreement over bill's effect on deficit	Substance: Disagreement over efficacy of provisions
Civil Debate Frame	Frame: "bipartisan bill," "working toward a compromise"	Frame: "bipartisan bill," "working toward a compromise"	Frame: "bipartisan bill," "working toward a compromise"
	Substance: Bundle of amendments attached to bill	Substance: Disagreement over bill's effect on deficit	Substance: Disagreement over efficacy of provisions

facets are the parliamentary tactics being employed by the respective parties, the program's cost, and the efficacy of the plan's provisions. Varying the substance of the debate in this way allows for greater generalizability from the experimental findings. It allows for the possibility that some Americans may view certain types of debate as legitimate (like disagreements over a policy's potential efficacy) and other types of debate as illegitimate (such as disputes over parliamentary tactics).

The tactics treatments provide minimal substantive information about the bill being considered. They provide the description of the bill that is common to all of the treatments regarding "vastly more spending" and note the party affiliation of the bill (Democratic—also common to all the treatments). The tactics treatments are focused on the attachment of a bundle of amendments to the bill. The amendments are described by the Democrats as "delay tactics" in the heated conflict version of the article, and described as a method of insuring bipartisan support in the civil debate version of the article. The tactics treatments are, therefore, designed to show the impact of partisan debate on policy attitudes in an instance where very little substantive information is available.

The spending and efficacy treatments provide a more moderate level of substantive information about the bill. These treatments give arguments for and against the passage of the legislation, describing the particular elements of the bill about which the parties disagree. In the two "spending" treatments, Republicans reject Democrat's claims that the proposal will decrease the deficit. In the two "efficacy" treatments, Republicans assert that some of the bill's provisions might do more harm than good because they are "risky" and "untested." The Democrats reject these arguments, claiming the plan will increase student test scores. All four of these treatments, therefore, describe the substance of the policy debate. The civil and heated versions of the treatments manipulate the tone of that debate. This allows the treatments to mimic real news articles about lawmaking, which typically outline the opposing views of those on both sides of a debate.

After reading the article to which they were assigned, all participants were asked to respond to several questions (the order of which was randomized). To assess perceptions of the policy-making process, respondents were asked: "Do you think the education reform process shows more that our policy-making process is working as intended, or more that our policy-making process is broken?" Respondents were also asked whether they supported or opposed the policy and where they would place the policy on a seven-point ideological scale.

Analysis and Findings: The Student Sample

One of the key assumptions on which the primary hypothesis is built is that many Americans view partisan conflict as a sign of dysfunction in the lawmaking process. I examine the veracity of this assumption by comparing the proportion of respondents that stated the policy-making process is broken in the heated debate groups with that of participants in the civil debate groups. Table 3.2 shows the results of T-tests measuring differences in proportions between paired treatment groups—meaning differences between the Efficacy/Heated group and the Efficacy/Civil group were analyzed, differences between Spending/Heated and Spending/Civil were analyzed, and so on. Asterisks indicate statistically significant differences in proportions between these paired groups.

Notice that in all cases, participants who received one of the heated debate treatments were more likely to view the policy-making process as broken than were participants who received one of the civil debate treatments. With the exception of the spending treatments, all of these differences are statistically significant. Overall, individuals who received one of the heated debate treatments were twenty-two percentage points more likely to view the policy-making process as broken than were individuals who received one of the civil debate treatments.

TABLE 3.2. **Proportion of Respondents Who Agree that the Policy-Making Process Is Broken, by Treatment Group (student data).**

Treatment	Tactics	Spending	Efficacy	Overall
Heated Debate	0.59	0.48	0.45	0.51
Civil Debate	0.22	0.38	0.27	0.29
Difference	0.37*	0.10	0.18*	0.22*

* Indicates 95% confidence.

TABLE 3.3. **Likelihood of Believing the Process Is Broken (student data).**

Variable	Coefficient	S.E.
Heated Debate Treatment	0.98*	0.22
Opposes the Bill	−0.50	0.33
Constant	−0.85*	0.17

$N = 367$; Pseudo $R^2 = 0.04$

* Indicates 95% confidence. Results are from a logit model.

I further explore the factors that affect attitudes toward the policy-making process by modeling the likelihood of a "broken" response as a function of exposure to heated conflict, and of opposition to the education bill. By including both of these variables in the model, I can test the degree to which attitudes toward the policy-making process are a function of the amount of conflict inherent in the process as compared with approval or disapproval of the legislation produced by the process. The results of the model are shown in table 3.3. They indicate that exposure to conflict is a statistically significant predictor of the belief that the policy-making process is broken, while opposition to the proposed bill is not. These findings provide strong evidence that heated partisan debate is interpreted by many members of the public as a sign of dysfunction in government, which leads to more negative evaluations of the policy-making process.

Conflict as an Ideological Cue

Next, I expect conflict to influence conceptions of the ideological content of the bill at the center of the debate. Individuals who receive one of the

TABLE 3.4. **Average Ideological Placement of Bill on a Seven-Point Scale (student data).**

Treatment	Tactics	Spending	Efficacy	Overall
Heated Debate	2.9	2.7	2.9	2.8
Civil Debate	3.5	3.2	3.2	3.3
Difference	−0.6*	−0.5*	−0.3*	−0.5*

* Indicates 95% confidence
Lower values indicate a more liberal assessment of the bill's ideology; higher values indicate a more conservative assessment of the bill's ideology.

heated conflict treatments should view the education bill's provisions as more ideologically extreme. In this case, because the bill is a Democratic one that increases education funding, "more extreme" means more liberal. To test this hypothesis, table 3.4 compares the average ideological placement of the bill by respondents on a seven-point scale, across treatment groups. Lower values indicate a more liberal placement of the bill and higher values indicate a more conservative placement of the bill. Paired T-tests are again used to assess statistical significance.

This analysis provides evidence in support of the ideological cue hypothesis. The T-tests show that across all the substantive treatments, respondents who were exposed to heated conflict evaluated the bill as more liberal than did respondents who received the corresponding civil debate treatment. On average, individuals who received a heated debate treatment assessed the bill as being half a point more liberal (on a seven-point scale) as compared with other respondents. Further, the influence of heated debate was strongest among respondents who received the "tactics" treatments, indicating that the presence of heated partisan debate might be a particularly strong ideological cue in instances where individuals have very low levels of substantive information about the bill under consideration.

To understand whether an individual will support or oppose a bill that they view as extreme, we need to take the individual's own ideology into account. Individuals with extreme preferences will support extreme bills. In the case of the education bill, strong liberals who are exposed to the heated debate treatment should place the bill closer to themselves, as the presence of debate should signal the extreme (very liberal) nature of the bill. Both moderates and conservatives should place the bill further from themselves on the ideological spectrum when it is associated with heated debate.

To test this hypothesis, I first generate a variable that measures the absolute value of the distance between the individual's placement of the bill on a seven-point ideological scale and the individual's placement of him or herself on the same scale (which was assessed with the pretreatment questionnaire). The variable has a mean of 1.6 and ranges from zero to five with a standard deviation of 1.2. I then model this distance as a function of exposure to heated debate separately for strong liberals (respondents who placed themselves at one or two on the seven-point scale), strong conservatives (respondents who placed themselves at six or seven on the seven-point scale), and all other respondents. Exposure to conflict is measured with a dummy variable that indicates whether the respondent received one of the three heated debate treatments. These models allow me to assess how exposure to conflict differently affected the perceived closeness of the bill to liberals and conservatives. Strong liberals should view the bill as being closer to themselves when they receive a conflict treatment while strong conservatives should view the bill as being farther from themselves.

Table 3.5 displays the results of the models. The first model indicates that strong liberals who were exposed to partisan conflict placed the bill about four-tenths of a point closer to themselves (on the seven-point scale) than did strong liberals who were not exposed to heated debate. This is indicated by the negative, statistically significant coefficient on the "heated debate" variable. In contrast, the coefficient on the "heated debate" variable is not significant for strong conservatives or "others" (although both coefficients are positive, as expected). These findings provide mixed support for my hypothesis. The belief that bills associated with conflict are ideologically extreme caused strong liberals to place the

TABLE 3.5. **Absolute Value of Distance Between Ideological Self-Placement and Placement of Bill (student data).**

Treatment	Strong Liberals	Strong Conservatives	Others
Heated Debate	−0.42*	0.22	0.11
	(0.17)	(0.18)	(0.13)
Constant	1.34*	2.97*	1.14*
	(0.13)	(0.13)	(0.09)
N	95	84	185
R^2	0.06	0.02	<0.01

* Indicates 95% confidence. Results are from OLS models.

bill closer to themselves when it was associated with conflict. However, strong conservatives and more moderate individuals who were exposed to debate did not place the bill further from themselves than they otherwise would have.

The Effect of Conflict on Policy Support

The ultimate goal of the experiment is to assess the impact of exposure to heated partisan debate on policy opinions. Toward that end, table 3.6 compares the proportion of respondents who stated support for the education bill across treatment groups. Paired T-tests are again used to assess statistical significance. Overall, 69% of respondents who received a civil debate treatment supported the bill as compared with just 52% of respondents given a heated debate treatment—a difference of seventeen percentage points. This finding provides support for the primary hypothesis, which states that the association of a policy with heated debate will result in decreased support for it.

Looking at the paired, substantive treatment groups, 73% of the respondents in the efficacy/civil debate group supported the bill. The same percentage of respondents supported the bill in the tactics/civil debate group. Support among respondents who received the heated debate version of those treatments fell to 50% and 48% respectively—a precipitous decrease in support.

The difference in support between the heated and civil versions of the spending treatment is much smaller (four percentage points) and is not statistically significant, although the difference is in the expected direction. Interestingly, support for the bill is highest among those who received the spending/heated debate treatment as compared with any of

TABLE 3.6. **Proportion of Respondents Who Support the Bill (student data).**

Treatment	Tactics	Spending	Efficacy	Overall
Heated Debate	0.48	0.58	0.50	0.52
Civil Debate	0.73	0.62	0.73	0.69
Difference	−0.25*	−0.04	−0.23*	−0.17*

* Indicates 95% confidence.

TABLE 3.7. **Proportion of Respondents Who Support the Education Bill, by Party (student data).**

Treatment	Independents	Democrats	Republicans	Overall
Heated Debate	0.49	0.76	0.32	0.52
Civil Debate	0.64	0.84	0.63	0.69
Difference	−0.15*	−0.08	−0.31*	−0.17*

* Indicates 95% confidence
The sample contains 130 self-identified independents, 112 self-identified Democrats, and 147 self-identified Republicans

the other heated debate treatments. It seems that partisan conflict over spending and the deficit is less likely to tamp down support for legislation than is debate on other topics. This suggests that debate over government spending may be seen as more legitimate than are other substantive topics of debate.

In table 3.7, I explore the degree to which the respondent's own party affiliation affects their view of the debate surrounding the legislation. One alternative explanation for the lower levels of support observed among recipients of the conflict frame is that the frame may function as a partisan cue. We might expect Republicans who know there is strong Republican opposition to a piece of legislation in Congress to side with their party by rejecting the bill. Conversely, we might expect Democrats to support legislation at higher rates when they know Republicans strongly object to it. The conflict frame may, therefore, function as a party cue, signaling the party's stance on the legislation to its members.[3] If so, the conflict frame should have the biggest impact on partisans. We would not expect effects on individuals who do not affiliate with either of the major parties.

To assess the degree to which this type of partisan cue taking is evident, I examine the impact of the conflict frame separately on Democrats, Republicans, and Independents (see table 3.7). I find that the impact of the conflict frame is strongest among Republicans—there is a thirty-one-percentage point decrease in support for the bill among Republicans who are given a heated debate treatment, suggesting some degree of partisan cue taking. However, support for the education bill also decreases among Independents and Democrats given the heated debate treatment. For Independents, the fifteen-point decrease in support is statistically significant. For Democrats, the eight-point decrease in support is not significant; however, I find no evidence that Democrats are more likely to support legislation that has strong Republican opposition. These findings support the assertion that the conflict frame is more than just a party cue. It suppresses support for legislation across the electorate. I further assess the influence of party affiliation on support for the bill in the model below.

Modeling Policy Support as a Function of Exposure to Conflict

Thus far, we have seen evidence in support of the hypothesis that exposure to conflict affects policy attitudes directly, and support for the hypothesis that conflict affects attitudes indirectly (by causing citizens to alter their placement of the bill on the ideological spectrum). As a means of testing these hypotheses against one another, I model the likelihood of support for the education bill as a function of exposure to conflict and the distance between the ideological placement of the bill and the individual's ideological self-placement. I also control for the respondent's partisan affiliation.

If conflict has a direct effect on policy attitudes, the coefficient on the conflict variable should be negative and statistically significant. If exposure to conflict affects policy attitudes indirectly, the coefficient on the ideology variable should be negative and statistically significant. If conflict affects policy attitudes both directly and indirectly, we should see the coefficients for both variables attain statistical significance.[4]

Table 3.8 displays the results of the logistic regression model. The coefficient on the conflict variable is negative and statistically significant,

TABLE 3.8. **Support for the Education Bill (student data).**

Variable	Coefficient	Std. Error
Heated Debate	−0.84*	0.23
Absolute Value of Distance between Respondent Ideology and Bill Ideology	−0.32*	0.12
Democrat	1.14*	0.31
Republican	0.02	0.30
Constant	1.11*	0.28

N = 364; Pseudo R^2 = 0.11

* Indicates 95% confidence. Results are from a logit model.

indicating that the association of a bill with heated conflict lowers support for it. The coefficient on the ideology variable is also negative and statistically significant, indicating that individuals who place the bill further from themselves on the ideological spectrum are less likely to support it. These findings show that conflict has both a direct and an indirect effect on policy support. I also find that Democrats are more likely to support the bill than are others; however, the Republican dummy variable fails the significance test. (This failure might be due to the high level of correlation between the Republican variable and the ideology variable. The correlation coefficient for the two is 0.58.)

To help interpret the substantive significance of the coefficients, I have calculated predicted probabilities based on the regression results. The top portion of fig. 3.1 shows the impact of the conflict treatment on the predicted probability of support for the education bill among Democrats, Independents, and Republicans, respectively. These probabilities were calculated while holding the ideological distance variable at its mean (1.60). Of those who were exposed to heated debate, the probability of support for the education bill was fourteen percentage points lower among Democrats, twenty-one percentage points lower among Independents, and twenty percentage points lower among Republicans. These finding provide strong evidence that exposure to partisan conflict has a direct, negative, substantively meaningful impact on policy attitudes. This effect depresses support among Democrats, Republicans, and Independents alike.

The bottom portion of fig. 3.1 shows the probability of support for different values of the ideological distance measure. The first value, 1.6, is the average distance between respondents and the bill. The second value is the average plus one standard deviation. For both values of the ideological distance variable, predicted probabilities were calculated for an Independent who received the civil debate treatment (as a way of holding these factors constant). The probability of support falls from .65 to .56 based on a one standard deviation increase in perceived ideological distance—a difference of nine percentage points. The predicted probabilities, therefore, indicate that perceived ideological distance plays an important role in shaping policy support. Because we have seen that exposure to conflict influences this perceived distance, we can conclude that conflict has both a direct and indirect effect on policy attitudes and that both of these effects are substantively significant. With the student data, however, I am not able to parse out whether the direct effect is

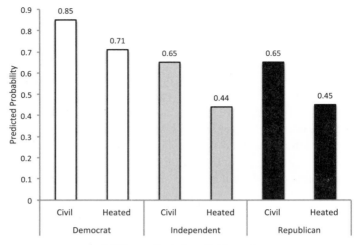

(a) Direct effect of conflict by party

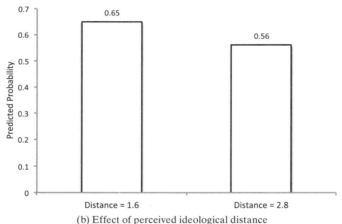

(b) Effect of perceived ideological distance

FIG. 3.1. Predicted Probability of Support for Education Bill (Student Data).

Note: Predicted probabilities are calculated for Independents unless otherwise specified. The ideological difference variable is held at its mean unless otherwise specified.

more prevalent among political novices and the indirect effect is more
prevalent among political sophisticates. This is because all respondents
in the sample have similar levels of knowledge about politics (all were
enrolled in introductory political science courses). To examine such differences, I must rely on the CCES data.

Replication with CCES Data

The main findings from the preceding analysis were replicated using a national adult sample as part of the 2012 CCES. The research design was altered slightly for this second administration. First, the low-information "tactics" treatments were omitted. These treatments had the strongest effects on attitudes among participants in the student sample. With the CCES data, only the spending and efficacy treatments are used, creating a more focused, harder test of the conflict hypothesis. Second, the remaining treatments were lightly edited to remove descriptions of conflict from the body of the news articles. After editing, descriptions of conflict appear in the opening two sentences and the closing sentence only—making the bodies of the corresponding paired treatments identical. Again, this change was intended to create a harder test of the conflict hypothesis. Third, respondents who believed the policy-making process was broken were asked a follow-up question that explored the reasons for this belief. The question was designed to test the assumption that political novices will view debate as a waste of time and as a sign that lawmakers are pursing their own political interests rather than the public good. Lastly, I added a control condition wherein the respondents were not asked to read a vignette or give an opinion on a policy—they were simply asked for their views on the policy-making process. This allows me to assess baseline levels of animosity toward the policy-making process that were not influenced by the content of the experimental treatments. This was useful because the experiment was conducted during a period of intense partisan debate (the lead-up to the 2012 presidential election), meaning levels of disapproval of the political process might have been especially high.

In fact, I do find that most CCES participants believed the policy-making process was broken. Roughly 80% of all respondents held this view, as compared with roughly 40% of the student sample. In addition to the difference in the timing of the two surveys, this discrepancy seems partially due to differences in the demographics of the samples. In particular, the average age of a CCES respondent was fifty-three, and older adults are more likely to hold cynical views about government than are younger ones. Among the college-aged CCES respondents (those between eighteen and twenty-two), just 63% believed the process was broken. Because of the higher average age of the respondents and because the CCES participants had undoubtedly been exposed to real world campaign coverage that employed the conflict frame, most respondents already believed the policy-making process was broken before they received one of the experimental treatments. Comparing the responses of individuals in the control group with those in the heated and civil treatment groups confirms this. There was not a significant difference between the control group and any of the treatment groups. Most individuals were already so unhappy with the policy-making process that exposure to additional political conflict did not change their attitudes toward it. Neither did exposure to a single article about bipartisan cooperation.

While attitudes toward the policy-making process varied little between subjects, the reasons why individuals held this negative view varied considerably. Participants were given four response options and asked to choose the one that best described why they believed recent debate showed that the policy-making process in Washington was broken. Two of the responses were designed to capture the belief that debate signifies misplaced priorities among lawmakers: "Politicians are more interested in advancing their careers than doing what is best for the country," and "time spent debating could be better spent actually fixing our nation's problems." Thirty-nine percent of participants chose the former and 26% chose the latter response. A third response option was designed to capture the sentiment that individuals simply wanted to see more cooperation on Capitol Hill: "Elected leaders are working against each other rather than together." This response was selected by roughly 12% of respondents. Finally, to assess whether participants view debate through an ideological lens, respondents were also given a response option that states: "Politicians will stick to their ideological principles no matter the consequences for the country." Twenty-three percent of participants chose this response.

In examining the source of this variation, I am most interested in whether beliefs about the policy-making process vary systematically with level of political sophistication—as my theory suggests it will. I expect political sophisticates to view debate through an ideological lens and novices to view debate as a sign of misplaced priorities. To test this, I measure political sophistication with two variables. The first measures attainment of a college degree—as individuals with more years of formal education should know more about the lawmaking process and the ideological differences between the parties. The second variable is designed to identify "ideologues"—those whose policy preferences are guided by an ideological worldview (Converse 1964). To construct the measure, I employ a battery of seven questions that gauge support for legislation recently considered in Congress, such as the Ryan Budget Plan, the repeal of Don't Ask, Don't Tell, and the construction of the Keystone Pipeline. For each bill, I recorded whether the individual held a liberal or conservative policy position. For instance, support for the Keystone Pipeline constitutes a conservative position whereas opposition constitutes a liberal one.[5] I then assessed the level of consistency of preferences across policy topics. Individuals who chose the liberal position six or seven times (out of seven) and individuals who chose the conservative position six or seven times are coded as respondents with consistent, ideologically based policy preference. The measure also indicates a high level of awareness about current political issues, as it requires individuals to know enough about each of the seven bills to correctly identify the liberal and conservative positions on each. For this reason, the indicator is a robust measure of political sophistication.

I use a multinomial logit model to evaluate the influence of political sophistication on beliefs about why the policy-making process is broken. The ideological response option ("lawmakers will stick to their ideological principles") is the comparison category. This means that the results provided compare the likelihood of choosing the ideological response as compared to each of the other three response options.

The model includes two control variables. First, I include the respondent's birth year because of the relationship between age and political cynicism. Second, respondents answered two blocks of questions, one of which contained the experiment described here. The order of the blocks was randomized and I include the variable, "question order control," to account for this. The variable is coded as one for respondents who received the experiment block first and zero otherwise.

Table 3.9 displays the results of the model. It shows that individuals with consistent policy preferences are more likely than those without to choose the ideological response over each of the other three options. This is indicated by the negative, statistically significant coefficient on each of the three "ideologue" variables. These individuals view the lawmaking process through an ideological lens, as expected. Further, they believe that differences between lawmakers are genuine, in that they are based on ideological disagreements. Individuals without consistent policy preferences, however, are less likely to believe that commitment to

TABLE 3.9. **Why Do You Believe the Process Is Broken? (CCES data).**

Variable	Coefficient	Std. Error
Politicians are more interested in advancing their careers than doing what is best for the country		
College Degree	−0.19	0.20
Ideologue	−0.61*	0.20
Birth Year	0.01	0.01
Question Order Control	−0.06	0.19
Constant	15.08	12.44
Time spent debating could be better spent actually fixing our nation's problems		
College Degree	−0.88*	0.30
Ideologue	−1.24*	0.27
Birth Year	0.01	0.01
Question Order Control	0.23	0.26
Constant	−28.70	15.84
Elected leaders are working against each other rather than together		
College Degree	−0.23	0.21
Ideologue	−0.58*	0.21
Birth Year	−0.01	0.01
Question Order Control	0.13	0.21
Constant	−10.61	13.16

N = 794
Pseudo R^2 = 0.03

* Indicates 95% confidence. Results are from a multinomial logit model. The base category response states that politicians will stick to their ideological principles no matter the consequences for the country.

ideological principles underscores political conflict. These individuals are more likely to believe that politicians are self-interested, that they are working against one another, and that debate is a waste of time.

Individuals with a college degree are less likely than those without a degree to believe that "time spent debating could be better spent on actually fixing the nation's problems." This signals some awareness of the legitimacy of policy debate and the role that ideological differences play in shaping it. However, college graduates are no less likely than others to hold the cynical view that the policy-making process is broken because politicians are focused on their own interests and are working against one another.

This analysis lends support to the claim that political sophisticates and novices have different expectations in terms of what constitutes a properly functioning government. For political sophisticates, policy debate is a reflection of ideological differences among elites. When those differences prevent politicians from finding a way forward together, sophisticates come to believe the process is broken. But the political novice believes gridlock and debate signal corruption and inattention to the nation's problems. This is a more cynical view—one that suggests an overall negative perception of political debate. It is for just this reason that I expect exposure to debate to have a larger direct effect on the policy preferences of the political novice than the political sophisticate. Political sophisticates, on the other hand, should be more influenced by their beliefs about the legislation's ideology. In the next section, I examine the effect of exposure to conflict on these beliefs.

Political Conflict and Ideological Extremism

Table 3.10 compares the average ideological placement of the bill by respondents on a seven-point scale, across treatment groups. As with the student experiment, I expect respondents to view the bill as more ideologically extreme when it is associated with conflict—and this is precisely what I find. Respondents who were given the heated version of the efficacy treatment believed the bill to be .25 points more liberal than did those given the civil version of it. This difference is statistically significant at a level of 95% confidence. Respondents given the heated version of the spending treatment believed the bill to be .13 points more liberal than did those given the civil version of it (a difference that is in the expected direction but is not statistically significant). These findings comport with those from the student data. They show that the association of a bill with heated partisan conflict causes individuals to believe the bill is more ideologically extreme.

To show how this belief in the extremism of the bill influences the perceived distance between the individual's ideology and that of the bill,

TABLE 3.10. **Average Ideological Placement of Bill on a Seven-Point Scale, by Treatment Group (CCES data).**

Treatment	Efficacy	Spending	Overall
Civil	3.47	3.30	3.39
Heated	3.22	3.17	3.19
Difference	−0.25*	−0.13	−0.20*

* Indicates 95% confidence

Lower values indicate a more liberal assessment of the bill's ideology; higher values indicate a more conservative assessment of the bill's ideology.

TABLE 3.11. **Absolute Value of Distance between Ideological Self-Placement and Placement of Bill (CCES data).**

Treatment	Strong Liberals	Strong Conservatives	Others
Heated Debate	−0.04	0.38*	0.04
	(0.16)	(0.18)	(0.14)
Constant	1.97*	3.50*	1.23*
	(0.11)	(0.13)	(0.09)
N	176	256	366
R^2	<0.01	0.02	<0.01

* Indicates 95% confidence. Results are from OLS models.

I again create a measure of the absolute value of the distance between the two. I then model this distance as a function of exposure to heated debate separately from strong liberals, strong conservatives, and all others. Table 3.11 displays the results of the three models.

The regression results show that for strong conservatives, the conflict frame had a significant effect on how far individuals believed the bill was from their own ideological preferences. In the absence of conflict, strong conservatives placed the bill 3.5 points from themselves on the ideological scale. When exposed to conflict, conservatives placed the bill an additional .38 points further from themselves on this scale (as indicated by the coefficient on the "heated debate" variable). These findings show that conservatives believed the proposal to be more ideologically extreme when it was associated with conflict, which in turn led them to view it as out of step with their own preferences. Strong liberals, however, did not place the bill closer to themselves when it was associated with conflict. On average, strong liberals placed the bill about two points from themselves on the ideological scale and this was not altered significantly by the association of the bill with conflict.[6] Again, these findings offer mixed evidence of an indirect effect of conflict on policy support.

Support for the Bill

My ultimate goal is to show how exposure to conflict shapes support for the policy being debated. Table 3.12 displays the percentage of respondents who stated support for the bill, by treatment group. Support for the bill was eleven percentage points lower among those who received

TABLE 3.12. **Proportion of Respondents Who Support the Education Bill, by Treatment Group (CCES data).**

Treatment	Efficacy	Spending	Overall
Civil	0.51	0.44	0.48
Heated	0.40	0.35	0.38
Difference	−0.11*	−0.09*	−0.10*

* Indicates 95% confidence.

the heated version of the efficacy treatment as compared with the civil version of the efficacy treatment. Among those who received the spending treatments, support was nine percentage points lower among those who received the heated version. These differences are statistically significant in both cases and support my main hypothesis. Support for bills associated with heated debate is lower than is support for identical bills not associated with such debate.

Next, I model the likelihood of support for the education bill as a function of exposure to conflict and as a function of the distance between the respondent's ideological self-placement and his or her placement of the bill. As with the student data, the respondent's partisan affiliation is also included as an independent variable. Unlike with the student data, here I am also able to examine the importance of political sophistication. I expect that exposure to conflict will have the largest direct effect on the policy opinions of those with lower levels of political sophistication and the greatest indirect effect on those with higher levels of sophistication. To test this, I run models separately for those with and without a college degree (again under the assumption that those with more years of education will know more about lawmaking). Table 3.13 displays the results of the models.

For individuals with a college degree, exposure to debate does not have a direct effect on support for the education bill. This is indicated by the failure of the heated debate treatment variable to attain statistical significance. This is true for respondents of all political stripes. As demonstrated by the predicted probabilities displayed in fig. 3.2, the conflict frame does not have a direct effect on support among Democrats, Republicans or Independents without a college degree. Perceptions of the bill's ideology, however, are important for these individuals. The farther sophisticates place the bill from themselves, the less likely they are to support it—as indicated by the negative, statistically significant coeffi-

TABLE 3.13. **Likelihood of Supporting the Bill (CCES data).**

Variable	College Degree	No College Degree
Heated Debate Treatment	−0.09	−0.52*
	(0.30)	(0.20)
Absolute Value of Distance Between Respondent	−0.65*	−0.32*
Ideology and Perceived Bill Ideology	(0.11)	(0.07)
Democrat	1.61*	0.91*
	(0.35)	(0.23)
Republican	−0.74	−0.98*
	(0.42)	(0.28)
Question Order Control	0.56	−0.61*
	(0.31)	(0.20)
Constant	0.68	0.72
	(0.37)	(0.23)
	N = 277	N = 521
	Pseudo R^2 = 0.30	Pseudo R^2 = 0.15

Results are from a logit model. * Indicates 95% confidence.

cient on the ideological distance variable. Generating predicted probabilities for this variable reveals that a move from the mean to one standard deviation above the mean (an increase of 1.6 points) results in a twenty percentage point decrease in the likelihood of support (see fig. 3.2). Just as expected, sophisticates' policy preferences are shaped by their beliefs about the bill's ideology. To the extent that heated debate sends a signal that the policy under consideration is extreme and out of step with their own ideological preferences, political sophisticates become less likely to support it. This finding bolsters the hypothesis that conflict will have an indirect effect on policy support among political sophisticates.

Returning to table 3.13, here we see that for individuals without a college degree, exposure to heated debate has a direct, negative, statistically significant impact on policy support. This stands in contrast to the findings for college graduates. Further, generating predicted probabilities reveals that for political novices, conflict depressed policy support for Democrats, Independents, and Republicans alike (see fig. 3.3). Exposure to heated debate decreased the probability of support by eleven percentage points among Democrats, thirteen points among Independents, and nine points among Republicans. As expected, conflict does more than simply amplify party cues by signaling which side of the fight each party stands on. Instead, individuals who know less about how government works view heated debate as a sign of corruption and misplaced

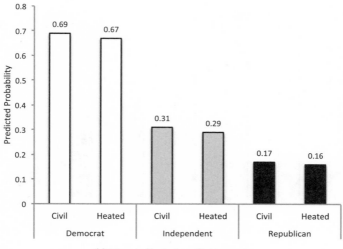

(a) Direct effect of conflict by party

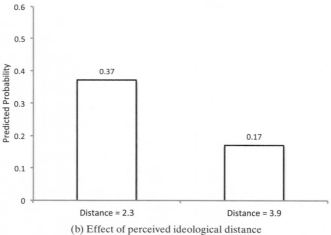

(b) Effect of perceived ideological distance

FIG. 3.2. Predicted Probability of Support for Education Bill for Those with a College Degree (CCES data).

Note: Predicted probabilities are calculated for Independents unless otherwise specified. The ideological difference variable is held at its mean unless otherwise specified.

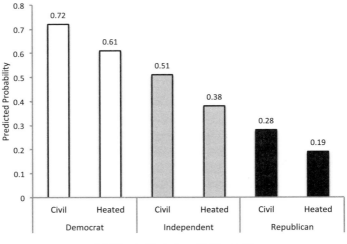

(a) Direct effect of conflict by party

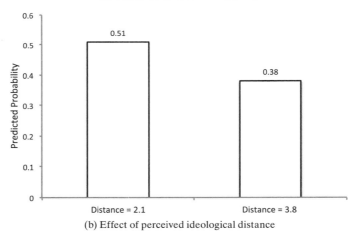

(b) Effect of perceived ideological distance

FIG. 3.3. Predicted Probability of Support for Education Bill for Those without a College Degree (CCES data).

Note: Predicted probabilities are calculated for Independents unless otherwise specified. The ideological difference variable is held at its mean unless otherwise specified.

priorities among lawmakers. As a result, they are less supportive of policies associated with debate, regardless of their own partisan affiliation.

The opinions of novices are also shaped by beliefs about the bill's ideology. A one standard deviation increase in the perceived distance between the individual and the bill results in a thirteen-percentage point decrease in predicted support for the bill (as compared to a twenty-point decrease among college graduates). The further these individuals place the bill from themselves on the ideological spectrum, the less likely they are to support it; however college graduates were more sensitive to this change than were nongraduates. As expected, the indirect effect of conflict is more influential for political sophisticates than political novices.

Summary of Findings

Taken together, the results from the two administrations of the experiment provide strong evidence supporting the theory advanced here. The results from the logit models estimating the likelihood of support for the bill show that respondents exposed to heated debate were less likely to support the legislation even when accounting for their party identification and their beliefs about the ideology of the bill. The mere association of a policy with intense conflict results in decreased support for that policy. This is especially true for individuals with lower levels of political sophistication. As shown with the CCES data, the direct effect of partisan conflict is stronger for the political novice than the political sophisticate.

Both administrations of the experiment also provide support for the ideological cue-taking hypothesis. When Americans see the parties locked in a standoff, they assume the bill under consideration must either be so liberal or so conservative that the parties are unable to find a compromise. Because few Americans favor ideological extremism and most reject policies that are far from their own moderate preferences, this belief can translate into decreased support for controversial legislation—especially among those who know more about how lawmaking works.

Through both a direct and an indirect mechanism, I have demonstrated that exposure to political conflict has a pronounced impact on individual-level policy support. However, as with any experiment, questions about the generalizability and external validity of the findings must be addressed. In chapters 4 and 5, I use observational, "real world" data to bolster the experimental findings presented here.

CHAPTER FOUR

Support for the Federal Marriage Amendment

The results of the controlled experiments I detailed in the last chapter provide support for my central thesis. They show that bills discussed using the conflict frame receive significantly less support than do those associated with lower levels of conflict. Yet, the tests leave questions about generalizability and external validity unresolved. To address those questions, I use a quasi-experimental design to examine the impact of exposure to conflict on policy opinions in the "real world." I examine support for the Federal Marriage Amendment (FMA) in 2004 and 2005, a period during which fifteen states considered ballot measures on constitutional amendments banning same-sex marriage. Residents of those states found themselves at the center of an emotionally charged debate and were the targets of well-funded campaigns vying for ballot measure votes. Residents of other states encountered demonstrably less debate about gay marriage. This allows for a comparison of attitudes toward the FMA among residents of states experiencing high versus low levels of political conflict.

The issue of same-sex marriage is well suited to an examination of the impact of political conflict on policy approval for several reasons. First, attitudes toward the substantive elements of the FMA are easily measured. Unlike complex policies with numerous provisions, the sole purpose of the FMA was to ensure that gay marriage would be prohibited nationwide. Further, unlike most domestic policies, the debate over the FMA did not include arguments about the plan's cost, the size of the government, or bureaucratic inefficiencies (factors that prior studies find can influence levels of policy support). In the absence of such arguments, I can cleanly measure and model support for the FMA as a function of exposure to debate and as a function of support for the policy's substance—the prohibition of same-sex marriage. Lastly, the marriage issue provides a particularly hard test of the hypotheses I outline. So-called "morality policies," like gay marriage, abortion, and stem cell research are shaped by first principles of religion or morality. Such policies are simple, nontechnical, highly salient, and elicit a gut response. In the vernacular of Carmines and Stimson (1980) they are "easy issues" and attitudes on these topics are thought to be more stable than are opinions on other policies. If exposure to debate can alter policy preferences on issues like same-sex marriage, it should be expected to influence attitudes toward non-morality policies as well.

The Same-Sex Marriage Case Study

Over the course of 2003 and 2004, the topic of gay marriage made headlines across the country. The series of events that focused national attention on the issue included actions taken by state and federal courts, Congress, the president, governors, and numerous state legislatures. Among the first of these was a March 2003 court ruling in Massachusetts that declared it unconstitutional to prohibit same-sex marriage in that state. Three months later, the Supreme Court of the United States also ruled on gay rights. The decision in the landmark *Lawrence v. Texas* case struck down a Texas sodomy law. The ruling had implications for similar laws in thirteen other states and, in effect, legalized sexual relations between same-sex partners nationwide.

These advances for gay rights achieved through the courts incited a backlash from legislators seeking to temper the influence of so-called "activist judges." At the federal level, Representative Marilyn Musgrave (R, CO) proposed a constitutional amendment that sought to prohibit gay marriage nationwide in May of 2003 (H. J. Res. 56 [108th]). The amendment was the second of its kind, but unlike the version proposed in 2002, Musgrave's bill gained an endorsement from President Bush (The Public Papers of the President 2004) and accumulated 131 cosponsors.

Across the country, fourteen states considered similar amendments during 2004 and early 2005.[1] While the federal amendment never stood a real chance of being enacted, the state amendments were all put to a popular vote during this period. Additionally, the state of Massachusetts convened a constitutional convention in the spring of 2004 that passed a measure prohibiting gay marriage and allowing civil unions for same-sex couples. That measure required approval by a second constitutional convention in 2005 before being placed on the ballot in 2006. Overall, the ballot measure campaigns and the protracted debate in Massachusetts created high-conflict environments with regard to the issue of same-sex marriage in fifteen states.

With the ballot measures came sophisticated campaigns waged by interest groups on both sides of the issue. Campaign committees spent approximately $13.4 million in an effort to sway citizen's ballot measure votes (O'Connell 2006). The bulk of that money was used on broadcast advertisements and direct mail pieces, which brought the debate into living rooms, kitchens, and bedrooms across each state (O'Connell 2006).[2] The local news media also followed the debate closely. Headlines like "Gay Marriage Vote Draws Big Guns" (Sullivan 2004) and "Barbs Fly over Gay Marriage" (Campos 2004) were splashed across ballot measure state newspapers from coast to coast.

The campaigns and news coverage generated by the ballot measures meant that residents of states considering amendments heard much more about the issue of same-sex marriage than did residents of other states. To illustrate this, I compare the difference in the amount of news coverage related to same-sex marriage printed in ballot measure versus non-ballot measure states between January 2004 and April 2005. I searched Lexis Nexis for news articles containing the terms "same-sex marriage" and "gay marriage" in the capital city newspaper or the newspaper from the most populous city in each state (depending on availability in Lexis Nexis) for all of the high-conflict states available. I repeated these searches with a sample of capital and major city newspapers from ten geographically and politically diverse non-ballot measure states. I then compared the average number of articles in ballot measure states with the average number of articles in non-ballot measure states.[3]

The search results are provided in table 4.1. They show that the average number of articles mentioning same-sex marriage in ballot measure states was about 515 and about 145 in non-ballot measure states. Thus, the issue received roughly three and a half times more news coverage in ballot measure states than in other states—a difference that a difference in means test shows is statistically significant.

Most of the articles about gay marriage included a description of the conflictual nature of the debate. I assessed this by combining the "gay

TABLE 4.1. **Number of News Articles Mentioning "same-sex marriage" or "gay marriage" between January 1, 2004, and April 30, 2005.**

State	Newspaper	Total Articles	Conflict Described
BALLOT MEASURE STATES			
Arkansas	*Arkansas Democrat-Gazette* (Little Rock)	480	83.10%
Georgia	*The Atlanta Journal-Constitution*	805	74.20%
Louisiana	*The Advocate* (Baton Rouge)	293	*
Massachusetts	*The Boston Herald*	652	*
Michigan	*Detroit Free Press*	10	70.00%
Missouri	*St. Louis Post-Dispatch*	733	69.40%
North Dakota	*The Bismarck Tribune*	134	64.90%
Oklahoma	*The Tulsa World*	559	64.80%
Oregon	*The Oregonian* (Portland)	793	*
Utah	*Deseret News* (Salt Lake City)	699	64.80%
NON-BALLOT MEASURE STATES			
Alaska	*The Anchorage Daily News*	94	83.00%
California	*The Sacramento Bee*	261	78.90%
Connecticut	*Hartford Courant*	0	NA
Florida	*Tallahassee Democrat*	1	100.00%
Illinois	*The State Journal-Register* (Springfield)	123	84.60%
Maryland	*The Capital* (Annapolis)	74	68.90%
Minnesota	*Star Tribune* (Minneapolis)	266	83.80%
Nebraska	*The Lincoln Journal Star*	75	70.70%
North Carolina	*The News and Observer* (Raleigh)	327	62.40%
Texas	*Austin American Statesman*	230	67.80%

Source: Lexis Nexis
* During the course of the data collection for this project, Lexis Nexis removed *The Advocate, The Boston Herald*, and *The Oregonian* from their archives. I was, therefore, unable to search these papers for articles that describe the nature of the same-sex marriage debate.

marriage" key words with conflict-oriented key words, such as "partisan," "battle," "feud," and "bitter" (words that appeared frequently in the "conflict-focused" reports identified in chapter 2).[4] The percentage of articles about same-sex marriage that contained these conflict-oriented key words is shown in the fourth column of table 4.1. On average, just over 70% of all the articles that mentioned same-sex marriage also included information about the conflictual nature of the debate. Put differently, when the news media discussed the issue of gay marriage, they almost always highlighted the controversial nature of the issue and the conflict surrounding it. Because residents of states considering ballot measures were exposed to more than three times as much news coverage on the issue of gay marriage, they were also exposed to a higher volume of information about the heated nature of the debate.

Ballot measure campaigns and local news coverage are two examples of the ways that residents of high-conflict states were exposed to information about gay marriage and the debate surrounding it. Residents of these states probably also received information from additional sources, such as social media and discussions with friends and relatives. By election day, even individuals who were not particularly attentive to politics were likely to have heard something about the same-sex marriage debate taking place in their state.

Changes in Support for the FMA over Time

Exposure to this debate at the state level had the potential to shape support for the Federal Marriage Amendment at the national level. In most cases, the wording of the state amendments was nearly identical to the wording of the FMA,[5] many of the same interest groups were involved in advocating for and against the state and federal amendments, and many of the arguments for and against the state and federal amendments were the same. Because of these similarities, the state and federal amendments will be linked in people's minds. If the debate at the state level caused people to view the ballot measure in a negative light—perhaps leading them to view the policy as a politically motivated, "wedge issue"—they were likely to view the federal marriage amendment in a negative light as well. I, therefore, expect residents of high-conflict states to be less supportive of the Federal Marriage Amendment in 2005 (following the period of heightened state-level debate over gay marriage) than they were in 2004.

Testing the Effects of State-Level Conflict

To test this hypothesis, I use a quasi-experimental design. I compare the change in the average level of support for the FMA in high-conflict states with the change in the average level of support for the FMA in all other states between March 2004 and April 2005. If my hypothesis is correct, there should be a larger decrease in support for the FMA in high-conflict states than in other states during this period.

The analysis is conducted using data from two ABC/Washington Post polls conducted in March 2004 and April 2005 that asked respondents, "Would you support amending the U.S. Constitution to make it AGAINST THE LAW for homosexual couples to get married anywhere in the U.S., or should each state make its own laws on homosexual marriage?" (ABC/Washington Post 2004 and 2005).[6] The polls were conducted by the same survey firm using the same methodology.

The benefit of using these polls is that their timing allows the opportunity to assess public opinion before and after the 2004 campaign season. In March of 2004, the referendum process was not yet underway in most states. Utah's legislature was the first to approve the placement of a marriage referendum on the ballot—the measure passed both houses on March 3rd. Yet, even in this early state, the popular campaign for the measure was in its infancy when the poll went into the field on March 4. In fact, in thirteen of the fifteen high-conflict states, the issue was decided on or after November 2nd, meaning that the height of the campaigns surrounding the measures came nearly eight months after the initial March 2004 poll.[7] Because the heightened debate that surrounded the initiative campaigns had yet to emerge, the timing of the March 2004 poll allows for a pretest or baseline measure of public opinion regarding the Federal Marriage Amendment prior to the referendum process.

By the time the April 2005 poll was conducted, residents of the high-conflict states had been exposed to the intense debate that accompanies the referendum process. Each of the 2004 ballot measures had been decided by the time the poll went into the field, as had the Kansas marriage amendment that passed on April 4th, 2005. Only Massachusetts had yet to hold a popular vote. The timing of this second survey allows for an examination of attitudes in referendum and non-referendum states following the conclusion of the campaign season.

Analysis and Findings

Fig. 4.1 shows the respective percentage of respondents who said they would support and oppose a federal amendment banning same-sex marriage, by year, and by residence in a ballot measure state. In 2004, roughly 40% of non-ballot measure state residents supported the FMA and roughly 60% opposed it. These percentages are not dramatically different in 2005. Following the conclusion of the campaign season, approximately 37% of non-ballot measure state residents supported the amendment and approximately 63% opposed it.

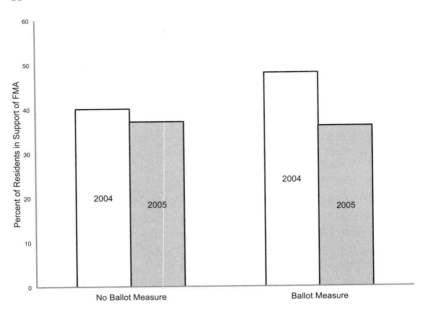

FIG. 4.1. Levels of Support for the Federal Marriage Amendment between 2004 and 2005 in Ballot Measure and Non-Ballot Measure States.

In ballot measure states, the change in support for the FMA is much larger. In 2004, about 52% of respondents opposed and 48% supported the amendment. By April 2005, however, the percentage of residents who supported the FMA had fallen to roughly 36%, a difference of nearly twelve points. This decrease in support for the FMA is roughly nine percentage points greater than the decrease in support in low-conflict states.

To determine whether the change in support for the FMA among ballot measure state residents differs significantly from the change among non-ballot measure states, a logit model is used to estimate the likelihood of support for the FMA. Here, the dichotomous dependent variable is coded one for respondents who support the FMA and zero otherwise. The key independent variables included are a year dummy variable (coded zero for 2004 and one for 2005), a dummy variable representing residence in a ballot measure state, and an interaction term that multiplies the two. The coefficient on the interaction term gives the difference-in-difference estimate for the treatment effect.

To measure support for the FMA's substantive provision—the prohibition of gay marriages nationwide—I include two dummy variables constructed from questions that gauge support for the legalization of same-sex marriage and civil unions. The first variable, "supports marriage," is coded as one for respondents who believe same-sex marriages should be legal and zero for all other respondents. The second variable, "opposes marriage," is coded as one for those who oppose same-sex marriage and zero for all other respondents. Support for civil unions but not same-sex marriage is the omitted category. I also include measures of self-reported ideology in the model because states considering constitutional bans of same-sex marriage are likely to have a higher proportion of conservative residents and a lower proportion of liberal residents as compared with other states. Further, support for states' rights is associated with conservatism. Conservatives who support states' rights might prefer to leave the issue to the states even if they oppose gay marriage.

With a policy like this one, that has a single substantive provision, we might expect support for the FMA to perfectly match up with attitudes toward the legalization of gay marriage. However, the cross-tab displayed in table 4.2 shows this is not the case. Of the 868 individuals who opposed gay marriage and civil unions, just 586 (roughly 68%) supported the FMA. Nearly 30% opposed it. Individuals who supported gay marriage were more unified in their opposition to the federal amendment. Nearly 83% of individuals who believed same-sex couples should have the right to marry opposed the FMA. Four percent stated they "did not know"—a share that is not significantly different from that of marriage opponents—leaving just 13% in support of the FMA.[8]

TABLE 4.2. **Comparison of Attitudes toward Same-Sex Marriage with Support for the FMA.**

| FMA Attitude | Support for Same-Sex Marriage | | | |
	Supports Marriage	Supports Unions	Opposes Marriage and Unions	Total
Supports FMA	n = 92	n = 159	n = 586	n = 837
	13.3%	31.7%	67.5%	40.6%
Opposes FMA	n = 572	n = 329	n = 257	n = 1158
	82.7%	65.5%	29.6%	56.2%
Don't Know	**n = 28**	**n = 14**	**n = 25**	**n = 67**
	4.0%	**2.8%**	**2.9%**	**3.2%**
Total	n = 692	n = 502	n = 868	n = 2062
	33.60%	24.30%	42.10%	100%

A tau-b test of association between the "don't know" dummy and an ordinal variable constructed from respondent attitudes toward same-sex marriage shows that the two variables are independent: Tau-b = .025; Z-score = .235.

TABLE 4.3. **Model A: Estimating Support for the Federal Marriage Amendment.**

Variable	Model A
Ballot Measure State Dummy	0.08
	(0.16)
Year Dummy	−0.16
	(0.13)
Year X Ballot Measure State	−0.39*
	(0.19)
Supports Marriage	−1.11*
	(0.16)
Opposes Marriage	1.40*
	(0.14)
Liberal	−0.41*
	(0.14)
Conservative	0.54*
	(0.09)
Constant	−0.68*
	(0.13)
N	2051
Pseudo R²	0.22

Notes: Results are from a logit model. Standard errors are clustered by state. * Indicates statistical significance at the level of 95% confidence.

The results of the model estimating support for the Federal Marriage Amendment are shown in table 4.3. Note that the coefficient for the interaction term "year x ballot measure state" is negative (as hypothesized) and significant at a level of 95% confidence.[9] This finding provides evidence that, when moving from 2004 to 2005, the likelihood of supporting the Federal Marriage Amendment declined among residents of ballot measure states to a degree that was statistically different from that of other states. The coefficients on the liberal and conservative variables are also statistically significant. Self-identified liberals are less likely to support the amendment and conservatives are more likely to support it than are moderates (the omitted category).

To assess the magnitude of the treatment effect in substantive terms, fig. 4.2 displays the predicted probability of support for the FMA by year and by residence in a ballot measure state. The first set of predicted probabilities (plotted in black) shows that the probability of support among ballot measure state residents dropped from nearly 43% in 2004 to approximately 30% in 2005—a difference of thirteen percentage points. The confidence intervals for these two sets of predicted probabil-

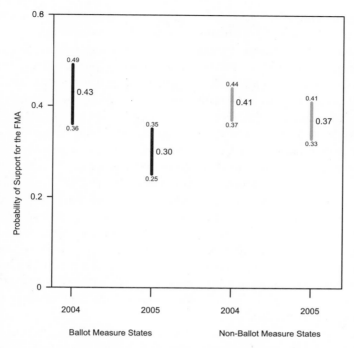

FIG. 4.2. Predicted Probability of Support for a Federal Marriage Amendment.

ities do not overlap, indicating that the change in support for the FMA is statistically significant. The probability of support among residents of non-ballot measure states (plotted in gray) decreased by just four percentage points and the change is not statistically significant—as indicated by the overlapping confidence intervals. These results suggest that the debate over gay marriage that accompanied the referendum process lessened support for the FMA in ballot measure states, while support in other states remained stable.

Alternative Explanations

The predicted probabilities shown in fig. 4.2 offer compelling evidence that support for the FMA decreased significantly between 2004 and 2005 in high-conflict states. But did this decline in support really stem from exposure to conflict? If so, I expect the decrease in support to be driven by political novices without strong preexisting policy preferences. As outlined in chapter 1, these individuals want lawmakers to work together to solve problems. Rather than championing a specific proposal, they favor a cooperative process that advances the public interest. When these Americans see lawmakers engaged in a protracted debated, they are more likely than those with strong policy preferences to view the conflict as a sign of dysfunction in the government and to reject policies associated with it. On the other hand, individuals with strong preexisting opinions—like marriage opponents—should be less susceptible to the direct effect of conflict. These individuals are more likely to view policy debate as a legitimate expression of ideological differences than a broken political process. Further, because they have a strong affinity for a particular policy, they can understand why others would also be willing to fight for a proposal they believe in. Individuals with strong policy preferences are, therefore, less likely to reject a policy simply because it is associated with heated debate. One way to suss out whether exposure to conflict truly underscored the decline in support for the FMA in ballot measure states is to examine what type of individuals changed their minds about the federal policy.

Such an analysis also allows me to test an alternative explanation for the observed change in support for the FMA. It is possible that people who opposed gay marriage were satisfied by the bans enacted at the state level and no longer saw a need for a federal ban after the referendum process. This hypothesis is plausible because the voters approved all of the state amendments considered in 2004.[10] This line of reasoning stems from Schattschneider (1960), who asserts that victors in a given venue will prefer that the issue remain within the jurisdiction of that venue—rather than risk having a favorable outcome overturned by expanding the scope of the conflict. In ballot measure states, marriage opponents became the "victors" when the constitutional bans were adopted, and their success at the state level may have dampened their support for the FMA. According to this alternative hypothesis, marriage opponents should drive increased opposition to the FMA in high-conflict states.

These two competing expectations are summarized in table 4.4, as is a final alternative hypothesis. The decrease in support for the FMA in ballot measure states could reflect a change in underlying levels of support for the policy's substantive provision—the legalization of same-sex marriage. After all, over the course of the ballot measure campaigns in high-conflict states, groups on both sides of the issue worked to dissemi-

TABLE 4.4. **Summary of Hypotheses.**

Hypothesis	Key Expectations
Conflict Hypothesis	Decrease in support for FMA in ballot measure states. Decreased support driven by those with weak attitudes.
Passage of State Amendments	Decreased support for FMA in high-conflict states driven by marriage opponents.
Substantive Considerations	Decreased support for FMA in high-conflict states driven by increased support for legalization of gay marriage.

nate persuasive messages about the issue. Generally, opponents of such bans argue that equal marriage is a right and that denying gay couples the opportunity to marry is discriminatory. Proponents claim that same-sex marriage poses a threat to heterosexual marriage and the traditional, nuclear family. Unlike policy debates in other issue domains (like social welfare policy, for example), arguments about the effectiveness of the policy, its cost, or its implications for the size of government are absent from the debate on gay marriage. Rather, the substance of the debate is aimed squarely at influencing individuals' underlying attitudes toward same-sex marriage. If residents of high-conflict states were persuaded by the substantive arguments of ballot measure opponents, we should observe increased support for the legalization of gay marriages and unions among these individuals.[11] This increased support for the legalization of same-sex marriage would then underscore the observed decrease in support for the FMA. In contrast, if exposure to political conflict led to the decrease in support for the FMA, no change in underlying attitudes toward the legalization of gay marriage is expected.

In the sections that follow, I test these alternative explanations for the observed decrease in support for the FMA in high-conflict states. I begin with an examination of attitudes toward the legalization of same-sex marriages. I conclude by examining which individuals changed their support for the FMA over time.

Did Support for the Legalization of Gay Marriage Increase?

If persuasive arguments against the state amendments were effective, we should observe an increase in support for the legalization of same-sex marriages and civil unions in the high-conflict states. Such a finding would suggest that substantive considerations, rather than exposure to conflict, underscored the decrease in support for the FMA.

To test this alternative hypothesis, attitudes toward the legalization of same-sex marriage are estimated with a multinomial logit model. The categorical dependent variable ranges from zero to two, with zero indicating opposition to marriage and civil unions, one indicating support for civil unions but not marriage, and two indicating support for equal marriage. The goal is to determine whether support for gay marriage or civil unions increased among residents of ballot measure states. Rather than assessing support for a specific federal policy—as in the previous model—here the dependent variable measures attitudes toward the legalization of gay marriage and civil unions generally. For this reason, while the key independent variables will be familiar, additional control variables must be included in this model.

The key independent variables are: a dummy measuring residence in a ballot measure state, a year dummy, and an interaction term that multiplies the two. The coefficient on the interaction term is the difference-in-difference estimate indicating whether any change in attitudes toward gay marriage among ballot measure state residents differs from any change in attitudes toward gay marriage among residents of other states. If the coefficient on the interaction term were positive and statistically significant, this finding would offer support for influence of substantive considerations.

As in the initial model (estimating support for the federal amendment), dummy variables for ideology are also included as covariates. Several additional factors are also likely to systematically influence opinions on gay marriage. First, the issue of same-sex marriage has become politicized—with conservatives and Republicans largely opposing gay marriage and liberals and Democrats largely supporting progressive marriage laws. For this reason, I include measures of party affiliation. Second, for many individuals, attitudes toward gay marriage are guided by religious or moral beliefs (Mooney 2000; Mooney and Lee 2000). Religious individuals, and Evangelicals in particular, are more likely to oppose same sex-marriage than are secular individuals (Pew Research Center 2006). For this reason, I control for self-reported religious identification using two dummy variables—one for Evangelical or Born Again Christians and a second for secular individuals. Religious individuals who do not identify themselves as Evangelical or Born Again Christians comprise the omitted category. Lastly, several studies document a correlation between higher levels of education and higher levels of tolerance toward people differing from one's self (Gibson 1987; Haider-Markel and Meier 1996; Seltzer 1993; Sullivan, Pierson, and Marcus 1982). For this reason, individuals with higher levels of education may be more likely to support equal rights for same-sex couples, including the right to marry. Level of education is controlled for with an ordinal variable coded as zero for individuals without a high school diploma, one for individuals with a high school diploma but no college education, two for individuals with some college (including a two-year or vocational degree), and three for individuals with at least a four year college degree.

The results of the multinomial logit model estimating attitudes toward same-sex marriage are displayed in table 4.5. The model uses opposition to same-sex marriage as the base category. The top portion of table 4.5 displays the coefficients for each of the independent variables on the propensity of an individual to prefer civil unions relative to opposing

TABLE 4.5. **Model B: Estimating Attitudes toward Same-Sex Marriage.**

Variable	Coefficient	Std. Error
Supports Unions, Not Marriage		
Ballot Measure State Dummy	−0.33	0.26
Year Dummy	0.64*	0.14
Year X Ballot Measure State	0.29	0.41
Liberal Dummy	−0.25	0.23
Conservative Dummy	−0.74*	0.18
Secular Dummy	0.18	0.24
Evangelical Dummy	−0.79*	0.18
Education	0.40*	0.07
Constant	−1.06*	0.20
Supports Marriage		
Ballot Measure State Dummy	−0.09	0.19
Year Dummy	−0.40*	0.14
Year X Ballot Measure State	0.03	0.38
Liberal Dummy	0.88*	0.17
Conservative Dummy	−1.27*	0.16
Secular Dummy	1.06*	0.30
Evangelical Dummy	−1.43*	0.26
Education	0.41*	0.07
Constant	−0.39*	0.16
N	1943	
Pseudo R^2	0.15	

Notes: Base outcome is "opposes same-sex marriage." Standard errors are clustered by state.
* Indicates statistical significance at the level of 95% confidence.

same-sex marriages and unions. Notice that the coefficient for the inter-active term "year X ballot measure," is not statistically significant. This indicates that, when moving from 2004 to 2005, residents of ballot mea-sure states became no more or less likely to prefer civil unions relative to opposing marriages and unions than did residents of other states.

The bottom portion of table 4.5 displays the coefficients for each of the independent variables on the propensity of an individual to prefer legal recognition of same-sex marriages relative to opposing same-sex marriages and civil unions. The coefficient for the "year X ballot mea-sure states" variable found here is negative and also fails to attain statis-tical significance. This indicates that, when moving from 2004 to 2005, residents of ballot measure states became no less likely than residents of other states to prefer same-sex marriage relative to opposing marriage and unions than did residents of other states.

In sum, I find no evidence that residents of high-conflict states changed their views on the legalization of same-sex marriage. Substan-tive considerations did not underscore the decline in support for the FMA in these states. This null finding strengthens the evidence support-ing the conflict hypothesis.

Which Individuals Changed Their Opinions?

The conflict hypothesis leads not only to the expectation that support for the FMA will decline among residents of ballot measure states, but also to the expectation that this decline will be driven by individuals without strong views on gay marriage. In contrast, if the decrease in support for the FMA in high-conflict states reflects a response to the success of the ballot measures, marriage opponents should drive the decrease.[12]

Individuals are classified as having weak attitudes if they hold a mod-erate position on gay marriage—supporting civil unions but opposing equal marriage. This is done because those who hold particularly *strong* attitudes (who we might call policy activist) generally support either equal marriage or oppose all recognition of same-sex unions—indicat-ing a link between the strength of one's attitude and the attitude itself. Marriage opponents are classified as those who oppose both gay mar-riage and civil unions for same-sex partners.

To assess whether individuals with strong views or weak views on gay marriage drove the decline in support for the FMA, the data are subsetted to include only the responses of high-conflict state residents. Logit models (models C and D) are used to estimate support for the FMA among these residents.[13] The key independent variables are: a year dummy variable, a set of dichotomous variables indicating the respondent's attitude toward the legalization of gay marriage, and a set of interaction terms that multiply the year variable times each of the respective attitude indicators.

Model C includes two attitude indicator variables (and the corresponding interaction terms): "supports marriage" and "supports civil unions." Model D replaces the "supports marriage" variable and interaction term with a variable indicating the respondent opposes gay marriage and civil unions and an interaction term that multiplies "opposes marriage" with the year variable. Measures of self-reported ideology are also included in both models.

The results of Models C and D are shown in table 4.6. Notice that the coefficient for the interaction term "supports civil unions x year" is negative and statistically significant in both models—as expected by the conflict hypothesis. This indicates a decrease in support for the marriage amendment among supporters of civil unions. The additional interaction terms fail to attain statistical significance in Models C and D, respectively. Support for the FMA is stable over time for both marriage opponents and marriage supporters.

To allow for an examination of the substantive significance of the interaction terms, predicted probabilities are generated and displayed in fig. 4.3. The first set of predicted probabilities shows the likelihood of support for the FMA among equal marriage proponents in 2004 and 2005. These predicted probabilities are not statistically different from one another. The second set of predicted probabilities shows the likelihood of support for the FMA among proponents of civil unions.[14] Between 2004 and 2005, support for the FMA decreased by twenty-four percentage points among individuals in this group. This change is both substantively large and statistically significant, as indicated by the fact that the confidence intervals for the two predictions do not overlap. This finding supports the conflict hypothesis—individuals without strong policy preferences were swayed by the tenor of the debate over gay marriage. Over the course of the contentious campaign, these individuals moved from supporting the FMA to opposing it.

The last set of predicted probabilities shows the likelihood of support for the FMA among opponents of gay marriage in 2004 and 2005. The

TABLE 4.6. **Models C & D: Likelihood of Support for the FMA in Ballot Measure States.**

Variable	Model C	Model D
Year	−0.46*	−0.29
	(0.21)	(0.29)
Supports Civil Unions	−.70*	1.93*
	(0.28)	(0.43)
Supports Civil Unions X Year	−1.05*	−1.22*
	(0.59)	(0.55)
Supports Marriage	−2.70*	—
	(0.35)	—
Supports Marriage X Year	0.22	—
	(0.42)	—
Opposes Marriage	—	2.64*
	—	(0.30)
Opposes Marriage X Year	—	−0.18
	—	(0.37)
Liberal	−0.31	−0.32
	(0.31)	(0.32)
Conservative	0.48*	0.53*
	(0.21)	(0.22)
Constant	.71*	−1.94*
	(0.23)	(0.21)
AIC	588	594
N	537	545

Standard errors (in parentheses) are clustered by state and bootstrapped.
* Indicates statistical significance at the level of 95% confidence.

change in support among these individuals was not statistically significant, casting doubt on the idea that the success of the state marriage amendments was responsible for the decrease in support for the FMA. In sum, individuals with relatively weak attitudes toward gay marriage drove the decrease in support for the FMA in high conflict states, as expected by the conflict hypothesis.

Conclusion

The findings presented here bolster the experimental findings outlined in chapter 3. They show that exposure to heated debate can depress policy support in the real world, where citizens receive information about policies from numerous sources. They also show that some individuals are more susceptible than others to the influence of the conflict frame. Individuals with strong policy preferences tend to hold fast to

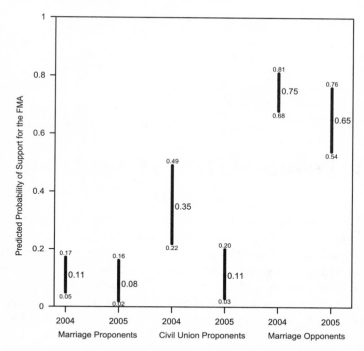

FIG. 4.3. Predicted Probability of Support for the FMA in High-Conflict States.

those preferences, even in the face of a well-publicized debate. But those with weaker preferences respond systematically to contentious deliberations—turning against the policy under debate over time.

Next, I use two additional case studies to further explore the effects of exposure to conflict, substantive support, and political sophistication on policy opinion. I show that, regardless of public support for a policy's provisions, the presence of partisan conflict can lead to a public backlash.

CHAPTER FIVE

The Politics of Health Care Reform

Unlike the case of gay marriage described in the last chapter, many of the policy debates that capture public attention center on proposed laws that are complex and multifaceted. Omnibus crime, farm, and economic packages, for instance, bundle hundreds of specific policy provisions together. Members of the public who want to understand these lengthy documents, filled with legalize and technical jargon, are almost entirely dependent upon the analyses provided by the news media. They turn to news reports to learn what the most important provisions of the bills are, what the effects of those provisions will be, how much they will cost, and what the passage of the plans will mean for themselves and their families. The choices reporters make in deciding which elements of the bills to highlight and how to frame the policy debates surrounding them necessarily shape public opinion on these types of "hard" issues.

Health care reform is just such a complex issue, one that has appeared on the political agendas of almost every president to serve since the end of the Second World War. During the postwar period, we have seen policy successes, such as the creation of Medicare, Medicaid, SCHIP, and the passage of the Patient Protection and Affordable Care Act, as well as failed attempts at reform during the Presidency's of Truman, Nixon, Carter, and Clinton. I will examine the dynamics of media coverage and public opinion toward two of these reform plans, the Health Security Act proposed by President Clinton and the Affordable Care Act signed into law by President Obama.

A great deal of excellent scholarship has examined both of these cases in-depth. Rather than duplicating that work, I focus narrowly on

how the two policy debates were portrayed in the press and the disconnect between the public's support for the substance of the two bills and
their opposition to the reform packages as a whole. I show that in both
instances, the media's focus on the contentious lawmaking process led
many members of the public to believe legislators were pursing their own
political interests rather than the public good. For individuals who knew
little about the legislative process, the belief that lawmakers were playing politics dramatically increased the likelihood of opposition to both
the Clinton plan and the ACA.

The Clinton Reform Plan

With the benefit of hindsight, many scholars and members of the press
have claimed that President Clinton faced an arduous, uphill battle for
health reform from the very start. Several factors contribute to this view.
First, President Clinton was elected by a plurality, not a majority of voters, meaning he lacked a mandate to pursue Democratic reforms in
Washington. Second, his health care plan was developed over a period
of several months behind closed doors with little input from Congressional leaders. This led to a third problem—the market-based reform
plan developed by the White House (under the leadership of the First
Lady) took a centrist approach and included few of the specific policy
provisions traditionally favored by Democrats.[1] Rather than calling for
a single-payer plan or offering a government-sponsored insurance option, the Health Security Act encouraged private insurance providers to
compete for customers in a system that regulated costs and required universal coverage. Democrats in Congress supported the goal of extending
health coverage to all Americans, but they were skeptical of the conservative approach Clinton outlined for achieving that goal (Zelman 1994).
Instead of backing the Administration's plan, members of President
Clinton's own party saw his bill "as grist for protracted bargaining over
this or that provision, and as fodder for infinitely complicated legislative
maneuvering" (Skocpol 1995, 73).

On top of all of this, President Clinton was not able to devote his full
attention to health reform. Instead, he split his focus with another piece
of legislation that put him at odds with many members of his own party—
the ratification of the North American Free Trade Agreement. The first-

term president was also distracted by a sluggish economy still emerging from recession, by crises in Somalia and Bosnia, and by the Whitewater scandal, which tarnished his personal image.

Each of these factors created obstacles to the passage of the Health Security Act, but the plan's demise was neither swift nor a forgone conclusion when the debate began early in 1993. For every impediment to passage there was a countervailing factor. First and foremost, Americans were calling for reform in large numbers. As described by Blendon and his colleagues (1995), health reform was a key issue for voters during the 1992 election and became even more salient after President Clinton took office.

> Voters in the 1992 election ranked health care as the third most important issue in their presidential vote choice, behind the economy and the federal budget deficit. By the time President Clinton had taken office, health care was listed second among the issues that Americans most wanted the government to address, behind only the economy. In May 1993, nine in ten (90 percent) said that there was a crisis in health care in this country (Blendon et al. 1995, 12).

These levels of public support for reform suggest that while President Clinton lacked a broad political mandate, he did have a mandate to address problems in the health care system. Moreover, the public indicated broad concern not only with the cost and quality of their own health care, but with that of their fellow Americans. Jacobs and Shapiro (1994) demonstrate that the public push for health care reform was underscored by concern for the collective welfare of Americans. They show that most Americans were satisfied with their own care in the early 1990s, but had become increasingly worried that the care afforded to others was lacking. This concern for the well-being of others, in turn, underscored widespread public support for the Health Security Act's central provision—universal coverage.

Americans favored a system of universal coverage by wide margins (see table 5.1). Even at the end of the long fight over reform (in September of 1994), 74% said they supported such a system (ABC News Poll, 1994). Many of the plan's other key provisions were equally popular. Support for an employer mandate stood at 72% in September of 1994. Support for portable coverage stood at a whopping 88%. A provision guaranteeing that coverage could not be denied on the basis of a

TABLE 5.1. **Support for the Substantive Provisions of the Health Security Act.**

Provision	Support	Oppose
ABC News Poll, September 1994		
A system providing universal health coverage for all Americans	74%	24%
A federal law requiring all employers to provide health insurance to their full-time employees	72%	27%
A federal law guaranteeing you cannot lose your health insurance if you change jobs	88%	11%
A federal law guaranteeing you cannot be denied insurance because of a preexisting health condition	87%	12%
Harris Poll, March 1993		
Gradually imposing limits that will keep increases in health care spending in line with the rate of inflation	84%	14%
Would you support such limits even if some health care services would be harder to obtain?	61%	34%
Marttila and Kiley, March 1993		
Placing a limit on the price of prescription drugs	86%	13%
Placing a yearly limit on total private and government spending for all health care in the U.S.	57%	37%
Placing a limit on the rates that can be charged for health insurance	81%	17%
Placing a limit on the fees that can be charged by individual doctors and hospitals	82%	17%

The results reported from the Marttila and Kiley poll combine "strongly favor" with "somewhat favor" and "somewhat oppose" with "strongly oppose".

preexisting condition was favored by 87% of the public. A range of provisions designed to regulate health care costs also garnered broad support. The least popular of these measures was a "yearly limit on total private and government spending for all health care in the U.S."—57% of the public favored it.

In sum, President Clinton's political leverage on the issue of health care was grounded in popular support for reform. Early in his first term, the public's strong desire to see change implemented in Washington led political spectators to believe that some type of reform was inevitable. It also brought moderate Republicans, who were fearful of ignoring their constituent's demands, to the negotiating table. But public calls for solutions to the nation's health care problems quickly gave way to opposition to Clinton's complex plan. Despite continued support for the proposal's substantive provisions, public opposition to the plan itself swelled from roughly 30% in the fall of 1993 to more than 50% in the summer of 1994 (see fig. 5.1). Support for the plan fell from a high water mark of roughly

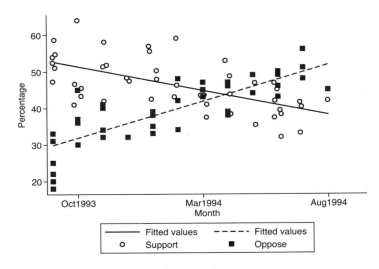

FIG. 5.1. Support for Clinton Reforms (1993–1994).

60% to less than 40% during the same period. This attrition of support was fueled by partisan attacks from the GOP's right wing and the media's portrayal of a bloody political feud over the bill.

Media Coverage and Public Knowledge

The long debate over the Health Security Act received unprecedented amounts of news coverage. Coverage reached the highest levels at the start and conclusion of the debate. From September through November of 1993, two thousand reports about health care reform appeared in print or on the air (West et al. 1996; Rosenstiel 1994). Coverage waxed and waned over the course of the next year, dipping to one or two hundred stories per month during lulls in the debate and spiking to several hundred reports each time a major development unfolded in Washington (Times Mirror Center 1995). As the debate entered its final phase during the summer of 1994, the issue dominated the news as it had during the fall of 1993 (Times Mirror Center 1995).

Several scholars have noted that the majority of this coverage focused on political strategies, the horse race, and the heated disputes between Washington elites (e.g., Cappella and Jamieson 1996; Jacobs and Shapiro

2000; Times Mirror Center 1995; Skocpol 1995). The Kaiser Family foundation, in conjunction with the Times Mirror Center, tracked the amount and content of news devoted to the Clinton plan as the debate unfolded. Their findings show that "the politics of reform dominated the coverage, while stories about the potential impact of reform on individuals and their families got ever-decreasing attention" (Times Mirror Center 1995, 1). The report goes on to state that "political infighting, counter proposals, and lobbying activities" were central features of news reports—findings that comport with the results of the content analysis detailed in chapter 2 (Times Mirror Center 1995, 2).

Opponents of health care reform anticipated this type of coverage (Jacobs and Shapiro 2000). Rather than an earnest debate on the merits of the plan, GOP leaders in Congress carefully crafted arguments designed to "demonize" the proposal by linking it to big government and an inefficient bureaucracy (Skocpol 1995). These sharp-tongued, partisan critiques attracted the attention of reporters who then amplified the disagreement in the press, just as Republicans predicted they would (Jacobs and Shapiro 2000).

All the while, members of the public continued to follow news of the reform effort closely. In October of 1993, 49% of the public said they were following "the Administration's proposals very closely" (Times Mirror Center 1993). Fig. 5.2 illustrates that levels of attention remained high throughout the debate. By the end of 1993, 60% of the public reported following news about the health care reforms "very" or "fairly closely." Nearly a year into the debate, in June of 1994, more than 70% of Americans reported this level of attention to the reforms. But even as they continued to tune in, many were dissatisfied with the content of the coverage provided by the press. A Brown University survey conducted in October of 1993 found that 48% of the public rated news coverage of the issue as either fair or poor. By August of 1994, that figure reached 64% (West et al. 1996, 42).

These low approval numbers almost certainly stem from the news media's fixation on the political contest and inattention to the substantive elements of the debate. This coverage left members of the public frustrated and confused about what the proposal would do if enacted. In fact, 77% of respondents to a national survey said they did not yet have a "a good understanding of what the Clinton health care plan will mean" at the end of the three-month media blitz that accompanied Clinton's unveiling of the proposal (CBS News/New York Times Poll, Nov. 1993).

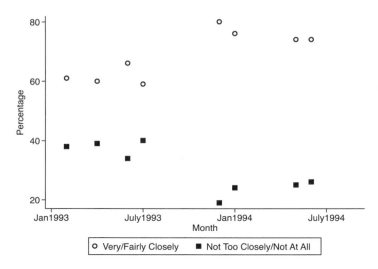

FIG. 5.2. How Closely Are You Following the Reforms? (1993–1994).

Similarly, an ABC News/Washington Post poll fielded the same month found that 55% of Americans felt they knew "little" and 31% reported knowing "almost nothing" about the president's plan.

Levels of knowledge were also low when it came to specific elements of the Clinton proposal. Fifty-four percent of Americans said they had never heard of "managed competition," the term that encapsulated President Clinton's approach to reform (Harvard School of Public Health Survey on Health Care Issues, Sept. 1993). Another 25% said they had heard the term but did not know what it meant. Forty-five percent of Americans said they had never heard of "health alliances"—a critical component of the Clinton plan—with another 32% saying they had heard the term but did not understand it. Only 31% of Americans had heard and understood the term "managed care."

Knowledge was perhaps highest on the subject of universal coverage. A Times Mirror News Interest poll (December 1993) found that 54% of Americans knew Clinton's reform plan guaranteed health insurance to all. Recall that 74% of the public favored such a provision, meaning that roughly 20% of the country favored universal coverage but did not know the Clinton plan would provide it. The Times Mirror survey also found that 44% of respondents knew the plan would allow workers to keep their insurance if they lost or changed their job, a provision supported by 88% of the public. The media's focus on the politics of reform and inattention to the substance of the plan, thus, had important ramifications for public attitudes toward it. The use of the conflict frame demoted the salience of information that the public viewed positively (the substantive details of the plan) and elevated the salience of information that the public viewed critically (the details of the political fight). This left many members of the public uninformed about fundamental components of the Clinton plan, and dissatisfied with the political process in Washington.

Attitudes toward the Process and the Plan

When President Clinton took office, levels of public cynicism were already high. For instance, in February of 1993, 29% of the public reported being "satisfied" with "the way the federal government works" (ABC News Poll 1993) (see table 5.2). A meager 4% reported being "enthusiastic" about the government. In contrast, 50% of Americans were dissatisfied with Washington and 16% reported being "angry."

Over the course of the health care debate, these negative attitudes toward the government only intensified. By the end of the debate in the fall of 1994, enthusiasm for government was down by half (to 2%), satisfaction with government was down three points (to 26%), and anger was up five points (to 21%). These statistics indicate that roughly one in five Americans was angry with the way the federal government worked at the end of the health care debate. One in two were dissatisfied.

Attitudes toward Congress also soured over the course of the debate (see table 5.3). From November of 1993 to September of 1994, the percentage of Americans who believed debate in Congress stemmed from "honest disagreement[s] about policy" dropped from 14% to 9%. Most

TABLE 5.2. **Feelings on How the Federal Government Works.**

Variable	Feb. 1993	Nov. 1994
Enthusiastic	4%	2%
Satisfied	29%	26%
Dissatisfied	50%	50%
Angry	16%	21%

Source: ABC News Polls.

TABLE 5.3. **When Members of Congress Cannot Agree, What Is the Reason?**

Variable	Nov. 1993	Sept. 1994
Honest disagreement about policy	14%	9%
Trying to score political points	78%	89%
Other	8%	3%

Source: The November 1993 data come from a CBS News/New York Times Poll. The September 1994 data come from an ABC News Poll.

Americans, instead, believed that when members of Congress could not agree, it was because "each side [was] trying to score political points." The share of Americans holding this view increased by eleven points to 89% over the course of the debate. Eighty-two percent believed members of Congress were more interested in serving their own political self-interest than in doing what was best for the country. When asked specifically about Congress's handling of health care, three-quarters of respondents said they disapproved of the way the legislature was handling the issue (ABC News Poll 1994).

These statistics illustrate just how widespread pessimistic views about Congress were in the fall of 1994. Further analysis reveals that majorities of Americans across a range of demographic groups—Democrats, Republicans, liberals, conservatives, old, young, black, white, rich, and poor—were dissatisfied with the lawmaking process. As shown in tables 5.4 and 5.5, none of these factors helped to predict cynicism. Of the demographic groups tested, the only significant predictor of beliefs about Congress was level of education (a categorical variable that ranges from zero to three). As level of education increases, Americans became more likely to believe that gridlock is caused by honest disagreement and less likely to believe it is caused by lawmakers' desires to score political points. Additionally, as education increases, citizens became more likely to believe members of Congress are interested in doing what is best for the country and less likely to believe lawmakers are interested in what is best for themselves politically. These findings support the theory I have advanced throughout—that individuals who know less about how government works are more likely to view debate as a sign that lawmakers are pursing their own political interests. Those who know more are apt to view debate as an expression of genuine disagreement.

TABLE 5.4. **Members of Congress Cannot Agree Because . . .**

Variable	Honest Disagreement		Both Sides Trying to Score Points	
	Coefficient	Std. Error	Coefficient	Std. Error
Education	0.27*	0.10	−0.20*	0.09
Democrat	0.35	0.42	−0.17	0.34
Republican	0.54	0.42	−0.29	0.35
Income	−0.05	0.06	0.04	0.06
Black	−0.34	0.39	0.23	0.32
Liberal	0.18	0.24	−0.12	0.22
Conservative	0.21	0.22	−0.31	0.20
Age	<0.01	<0.01	<0.01	<0.01
Constant	−3.20*	0.57	−2.51*	0.50
N	1453		1453	
Pseudo R^2	0.01		0.01	

Source: ABC News Poll, September 1994.
Results are from logit models. * Indicates P<0.05.

TABLE 5.5. **Most Members of Congress Are Most Interested in Doing What's Best . . .**

Variable	For the Country		For Themselves Politically	
	Coefficient	Std. Error	Coefficient	Std. Error
Education	0.30*	0.08	−0.27*	0.08
Democrat	0.45	0.30	−0.04	0.26
Republican	0.27	0.31	0.10	0.26
Income	0.04	0.05	<−0.01	0.05
Black	−0.31	0.29	0.14	0.26
Liberal	−0.14	0.18	0.13	0.17
Conservative	−0.33	0.18	0.32	0.17
Age	<−0.01	<0.01	<0.01	<0.01
Constant	−1.37	2.21	−5.30	8.35
N	1453		1453	
Pseudo R^2	0.02		0.02	

Source: ABC News Poll, September 1994.
Results are from logit models. * Indicates p < .05.

The Impact of the Process of Policy Opinions

To demonstrate the impact these negative views of the policy-making process had on opinions of the Health Security Act, I model opposition to the plan as a function of attitudes toward the process and attitudes toward the substantive provisions of the legislation. The data come from an ABC News Poll fielded in September of 1994. The dichotomous dependent variable is created from responses to the following question: "As you may know, it now looks like Congress this year will not enact the broad health care changes proposed by Clinton and the Democratic leaders in Congress. Do you think that's a good thing or a bad thing?" Roughly 54% of respondents said it was a "good thing" that the legislation was not going to pass. These responses are coded as one for "policy opposition." Those who believed the policy's failure was a "bad thing" were coded as zero.

Attitudes toward the policy-making process were gauged using a question that asked whether respondents thought, "Congress members are more interested in playing politics than in getting things done." Eighty-eight percent of respondents believed "playing politics" was a major reason more didn't get done in Washington. Note that the small amount of variance in responses to this question makes it unlikely that the dichotomous variable constructed from it will attain statistical significance. But, as I will demonstrate below, the belief that members of Congress are playing politics is an important predictor of opposition to the Health Security Act.

As described above and discussed in chapter 1, individuals who know less about how government works are more likely to view debate in a negative light. Those beliefs about the policy-making process then directly influence levels of policy approval in turn. On the other hand, individuals who know more are less likely to view debate as a sign of a broken system, and are more likely to view debate through an ideological lens. Moreover, these individuals should decide how much they like a policy based on its congruence with their own preferences rather than the association with conflict. As a result, political sophisticates should be willing to support a policy that has substantive provisions they like *even if they believe the reform is a product of politics*. For these reasons, I include level of education (measured as above) in the model as a proxy for political knowledge and I interact the measure with the "playing politics" variable. I expect to find that negative perceptions of the policy-making process have a larger impact on individuals with lower levels of education.

Support for the substantive elements of the plan is measured using responses to four separate questions that respectively ask about support for universal coverage, an employer mandate to provide coverage for all full-time workers, a guarantee that health insurance can not be lost if you change jobs, and support for a law that would prevent the denial of coverage on the basis of preexisting conditions. Control variables measuring political ideology, party affiliation, and level of income are also included in the model.

The results of the model are shown in table 5.6. Notice that attitudes toward the political process and education are statistically significant. An F-test for joint significance shows that the interaction term and its component parts are significant at a level of 95% confidence. These findings indicate that perceptions of the policy-making process shape policy opinions, but that political novices and sophisticates are differently affected by those perceptions. I discuss this finding in depth below. We also see that support for two of the four substantive provisions—universal coverage and the employer mandate—are significant predictors of policy opposition. Individuals who favor these provisions are less likely to oppose the Health Security Act. Support for coverage you can keep if you lose or change jobs and support for coverage for those with preexisting conditions are not statistically significant predictors of opposition. Given that these provisions were very popular with the public, their lack of statistical significance might reflect public ignorance. Because most Americans did not know the Health Security Act contained these provisions, support for the provisions did not influence opposition toward

TABLE 5.6. MODELING OPPOSITION TO THE CLINTON HEALTH REFORMS.

Variable	Coefficient	Std. Error
Believes MOC are Playing Politics	0.80*	0.35
Education	0.39*	0.16
Education X Playing Politics	−0.31*	0.17
Supports Universal Coverage	−1.16*	0.17
Supports Employer Mandate	−0.64*	0.15
Supports Coverage if you Change Jobs	−0.18	0.22
Supports Coverage for those with Preexisting Conditions	−0.05	0.20
Liberal	−0.46*	0.15
Conservative	0.33*	0.15
Democrat	−0.18	0.22
Republican	1.03*	0.23
Income	0.14*	0.04
Constant	−0.04	0.47

N = 1453
Pseudo R^2 = 0.20

Source: ABC News Poll, September 1994. Results are from a logit model. * Indicates $P<0.05$. A joint F-test shows that the interaction term and its component parts are significant at a level of 95% confidence.

the plan. The findings also show that, as expected, Republicans and conservatives are more likely to oppose the legislation while liberals are less likely to oppose it. Finally, individuals with higher incomes are more likely to oppose the legislation, all other factors being equal.

The predicted probabilities displayed in fig. 5.3 shed light on the substantive importance of the interaction term. For each level of education, separate probabilities are plotted for those who believe lawmakers from both parties are playing politics (plotted in black) and for those who do not (plotted in gray). The length of the line segment displayed indicates the degree of difference in the probability of opposition between the two groups of individuals.

The figure shows that as level of education increases, beliefs about the policy-making process shape policy opposition less and less. For individuals without a high school diploma, the probability of opposition to the plan is twenty percentage points higher (.56 versus .36) for individuals who believe members of Congress are playing politics—even when controlling for support for the substantive elements of the plan, party affiliation, ideology, and income. This difference is statistically significant and substantively large.[2] Among individuals with a high school diploma, the belief that members of Congress are playing politics also has a sizeable impact on the probability of opposition. Opposition is twelve percentage points higher (0.58 versus 0.46) among respondents who hold this view. But for respondents with some college, perceptions of the political process have a much smaller impact on opposition to the Health Security Act. Here, those who believe members of Congress are playing politics are just four percentage points more likely to oppose the president's plan and this difference is not statistically significant. Among those with a college degree, the results are even more striking. Here we see that those who hold the "playing politics" view are actually *less* likely to oppose the legislation, but again, the difference is not statistically significant. The findings indicate that the opinions of sophisticates are shaped less by their beliefs about the policy-making process and (presumably) more by their feelings toward the specific provisions contained in the legislation. For those with lower levels of education, however, beliefs about the motives that shape lawmaker's actions have a profound impact on policy approval.

Taken as a whole, these findings help to demonstrate the important impact that perceptions of the policy-making process can have on policy opinion. The news media's widespread use of the conflict frame crowded out information about the substantive provisions of the plan—informa-

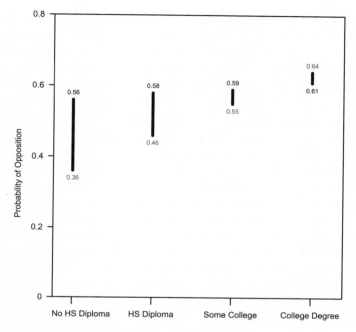

FIG. 5.3. Predicted Probability of Opposition to Clinton Plan.

Note: The predicted probability of opposition for individuals who do not believe lawmakers are playing politics is plotted in gray. The predicted probability of opposition for individuals who do believe lawmakers are playing politics is plotted in black. The length of the line segment indicates the degree of difference in the probability of opposition between the two groups of individuals.

tion that most members of the public viewed positively—and heightened the salience of negative information about the partisan "battle." For individuals with low levels of education, exposure to this negative information increased the probability of opposition dramatically. As a result, levels of opposition to the plan grew over time as the public heard more and more about the contentious debate. This pattern of conflict focused news and increasing policy opposition is repeated in the case of Affordable Care Act, detailed below.

The Obama Health Care Reforms

Like President Clinton, Senator Barack Obama made health reform a key feature of his 2008 presidential campaign. And just as it did in 1992, health care stood out as an important issue for voters. Nearly a third of individuals polled in December of 2007 said that health care was the top issue they would like to hear the presidential candidates discuss— making it the second most important campaign issue at that time (Kaiser 2007). On this key issue, voters believed Senator Obama would do a better job than would his opponent, Senator John McCain (Newport 2008). Voters also believed Obama would better handle the economy, energy, and taxes. These favorable public assessments helped Senator Obama win the presidency by a wide margin. He assumed office having won nearly 53% of the popular vote. He also ushered sizeable Democratic majorities into both Houses of Congress along with him.

The president's public popularity coupled with firm Democratic control of Congress seemed to perfectly position President Obama to fulfill his campaign pledge to make health care more accessible and more affordable for millions of Americans. But despite his electoral mandate, Obama faced two critical obstacles to a swift victory on health reform— an economic meltdown the likes of which had not been seen since the Great Depression, and a Republican minority determined to block the president's reform agenda.

Over the course of 2007, the economy slowed and by early 2008 the country had plunged into recession. The bad news mounted over the course of the year as financial institutions like Bear Sterns and Lehman Brothers failed, the stock market crashed, layoffs surged, and U.S. auto manufacturers teetered on the edge of bankruptcy. With grave economic news making headlines across the country, the state of the economy replaced health care in importance in the minds of many Americans. Between January and March of 2008, the number of Americans who viewed the economy as the country's most important problem nearly doubled, swelling from 18% to 35% (Jacobe 2008). Other Americans mentioned a specific aspect of the economy, such as fuel prices, unemployment, or the cost of living, as the most important problem. Combined, 55% of the public believed some facet of the economy was the most critical issue facing the nation in March of 2008 (Jacobe 2008). Upon taking office, President Obama had to adjust his priorities to account for these economic realities. Instead of health care, his first bruising political battle was over a massive stimulus package opposed by almost every Congressional Republican. The nearly $800 billion American Recovery and Reinvestment Act passed along party lines (picking up just three Republican votes in the Senate) and was signed into law on February 17, 2009.

With the public's attention on the economy, the attention of Congressional Republicans was focused on discrediting the stimulus package—by arguing the plan was a fiscally irresponsible government handout—and on denying President Obama another high-profile legislative victory (Skocpol and Jacobs 2012). To achieve the latter goal, the Republican leadership set its sites on health care reform, which President Obama declared "cannot wait, must not wait, and it will not wait another year," in a statement to a joint session of Congress on February 24, 2009.

The debate over the plan gained momentum slowly during the spring. President Obama convened a health care summit in early March and the Senate Finance Committee held an initial roundtable on health policy in April. By late spring, specific provisions of the bill were being debated in earnest and a proposal began to take shape. Using much the same language they had used to discredit President Clinton's proposal, Republicans wasted no time in attacking the fledgling plan as a government takeover of the health care system. Although the bill reported out of the Senate's Health, Education, Labor and Pension's Committee in July was a bipartisan one that included more than one hundred Republican amendments, publicly, the Republican party painted the bill as a big-government, liberal policy that was being strong-armed through Congress by the Democratic majority (Jacobs and Mettler 2011). The arguments about Democratic tactics gained credibility when, in late 2009, the public learned that Senate Majority Leader Harry Reid had tried to clinch Senator Ben Nelson's (D-NE) deciding vote by offering him $100 million in Medicaid funding.

Press Coverage of the Debate

The press followed the development of the health care debate closely, making it one of the most heavily covered stories of 2009 (Pew 2009c). Coverage spiked during the summer, with reports about health care reform comprising as much as 30% of the national newshole during a handful of weeks in August and September (Pew 2009c). This onslaught of news coverage coincided with an especially rancorous period of the debate. During the Congressional recess, many lawmakers held town hall meetings in their districts to discuss a range of policies. In several districts, these meetings attracted dozens, and in some instances hundreds of constituents who chose the meetings as forums to express their anger over the Democratic reform plan. Journalists rushed to cover the meetings and prominently featured accounts of the most hostile exchanges between constituents and lawmakers on front pages across the country. For instance, news outlets nationwide reported that members of the audience at a Lebanon Pennsylvania meeting shouted at, booed, and shoved Democratic Senator Arlene Spector (Shanahan 2013). Similarly, a Tampa, Florida, meeting generated headlines because hundreds of protestors who were not allowed in to Congresswoman Kathy Castro's town hall meeting stood outside the closed proceedings, "banging on the door," and shouting "tyranny" (Shanahan 2013). Across the country, Americans watched as discontent with the government spawned a new "Tea Party" movement and the battle over "Obamacare" became increasingly bloody.

This incivility extended to Capitol Hill as well. President Obama outlined his health care plan in a speech to a joint session of Congress on September 9, 2009. In the speech, the president attempted to refocus the debate on the substance of the legislation and tried to dispel popular misconceptions about the plan. While explaining that the plan would not extend health coverage to illegal aliens, the president was interrupted by Republican Representative Joe Wilson, who shouted "you lie" in response to the president's remarks. The next day, reports about the outburst dominated the airwaves. The following week, polls found that 83% of Americans had heard about the incident. Most Americans (53%) also reported a belief that the health care debate had generally been rude and disrespectful (Pew 2009d).

While these dramatic events catalyzed a wave of news coverage during the late summer months, throughout the debate, reporters sought out sensational storylines and concentrated disproportionately on conflict, political strategies, legislative tactics, and the horse race between political elites. Researchers at Pew's Center for Excellence in Journalism identified six major themes in reports about the health care debate. "Politics and strategy" was the dominant theme in a plurality of reports—40% of news reports were based on these aspects of the debate (Pew 2010a). Less than one quarter of all news reports focused primarily on descriptions of the proposed provisions of the various reform plans. Of those that did focus on the substance, "while outlining the elements of the proposals, [many of these reports] also focused on the political calculus for passage" (Pew 2010a, 8). Descriptions of partisan conflict were, therefore, pervasive elements of the coverage of health care reform, permeating even the reports centering on the substance of the Affordable Care Act. Just 9% of the coverage focused on the underlying issue—"the health care system itself, what works, what doesn't, what needs to be fixed and what is all right" (Pew 2010a, 7).

The American public followed these reports intently (see fig. 5.4). Over the course of 2009, a large majority—between 70% and 80%—said they were following the health care debate "somewhat" or "very closely." In fact, health care reform was the story followed most closely by the American public for twenty weeks during 2009 (roughly 40% of the year) (Pew 2009c). But just as during the Clinton health debate, members of the public were dissatisfied with the quality of the news they were voraciously consuming. Polls found that 70% of individuals believed news organizations had done either a poor or only a fair job of "of explaining the effect the proposals would have on people like [themselves]" (Pew 2010b, 4). Three-quarters of respondents said the news media had "done only a fair or a poor job of explaining the details of the proposal" (Pew 2010b, 4).

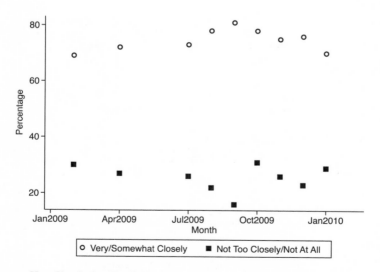

FIG. 5.4. How Closely Are You Following the Health Care Debate in Washington?

Perceptions of the Policy-Making Process

Public assessments of the debate itself were similarly negative. Nearly three-quarters of respondents surveyed at the height of the debate stated it demonstrated that "our policymaking process is broken," rather than working as intended (Kaiser 2010a). When asked to give a one-word impression of Congress in the days just prior to the House vote on the sweeping reform package that was ultimately enacted, the most frequent responses were "dysfunctional," "corrupt," "self-serving," and "inept" (Pew 2010c). Support for the legislation itself also fell over the course of the debate while opposition mounted. As shown in fig. 5.5, opposition to the plan peaked in late 2010 at approximately 50% with approval falling to roughly 40%.

These reactions from the public are not surprising when viewed as a reflection of the tenor of the debate and the media's portrayal of it. But they are surprising when attitudes toward the substantive provisions of the law are taken into account. Members of Congress were able to break the deadlock and enact landmark legislation that contained provisions supported by large majorities of the American public. For instance, 82% of Americans strongly or somewhat favored expanding

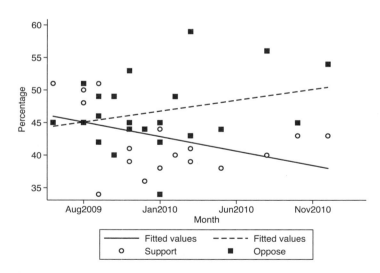

FIG. 5.5. Support For and Opposition to the Affordable Care Act.

Medicaid and SCHIP (a health insurance program for low-income children) (Kaiser 2009). Eighty percent strongly or somewhat favored requiring health insurance companies to cover everyone who applies for insurance, regardless of preexisting conditions (Kaiser 2009). Sixty-eight percent strongly or somewhat favored requiring all Americans to have medical insurance if those who could not afford it were given financial help (Kaiser 2009). And 67% strongly or somewhat favored tax cuts to help people buy private insurance (Kaiser 2009). When public opinion on these elements of the law is taken into consideration, the public's distain for the ACA and belief that the policy-making process was broken is puzzling.

The Influence of Process and Substance on Policy Opposition

To help solve this puzzle, I model opposition to the ACA as a function of individual's attitudes toward the policy-making process and toward the substantive provisions of the law. The model, which relies on data from a February 2010 Kaiser Family Foundation Poll, is constructed to be as similar as possible to the model estimating opposition to the Health Security Act.

Opposition to the ACA was measured using a question that asked, "As of right now, do you generally (support) or generally (oppose) the health care proposals being discussed in Congress" (Kaiser 2010b). About 45% of respondents stated they "strongly" or "somewhat oppose" the reform proposals. These responses were coded as one and all other responses are coded as zero. The key independent variable of interest, measuring attitudes toward the policy-making process, was created from a question that asked, "Do you think the delays in passing the health care reform are more about (Republicans) and (Democrats) having fundamental disagreements on what would be the right policy for the country, or more about both sides playing politics with the issue?" (Kaiser 2010b). Fifty-eight percent of respondents believed members of both parties were playing politics. These responses are coded as one and all other responses were coded as zero. Overall, roughly 24% of respondents believed delays were because of fundamental disagreements and 17% of respondents volunteered other answers (such as, delays are due to both politics and disagreement) or declined to answer.

As with attitudes toward Congress during the debate over Clinton's

TABLE 5.7. **Delays in Passing Reforms Reflect . . .**

	Fundamental Disagreement		Both Sides Are Playing Politics	
Variable	Coefficient	Std. Error	Coefficient	Std. Error
Education	0.19*	0.09	−0.10	0.08
Democrat	0.21	0.18	−0.08	0.16
Republican	0.25	0.19	−0.47*	0.17
Income	0.01	0.04	−0.02	0.03
Black	0.31	0.25	−0.25	0.22
Liberal	0.26	0.20	−0.03	0.18
Conservative	0.32	0.18	<−0.01	0.15
Age	−0.01*	<0.01	0.01*	<0.01
Constant	−1.41*	0.30	0.45*	0.26
N	1030		1030	
Pseudo R²	0.02		0.01	

Source: Kaiser (February 2010). * Indicates p < .05.

Health Security Act, cynical views predominated across a range of demographic groups in 2010. Table 5.7 shows the effects of education, partisanship, race, income, political ideology, and age on the belief that delays reflect fundamental disagreements versus political opportunism. Once again we see that as education increases, individuals become more likely to think delays in passing reform reflect fundamental disagreements over policy. (Education does not, however, have a significant effect on the belief that both sides are playing politics.) Along with education, age is also a significant predictor of cynicism—older Americans are less likely to believe delays are about fundamental disagreements and are more likely to believe both sides are playing politics than are younger Americans. Finally, with regard to political opportunism, Republicans are less likely to view debate as a sign that both sides are playing politics than are others (perhaps because they believe members of their own party are genuine in their opposition to "ObamaCare").

Clearly, level of political sophistication has an effect on how individuals perceive political debate and gridlock. Those who know less about politics are less likely to view debate as a reflection of genuine disagreement over policy. Political novices should, therefore, be more influenced by conflict-focused news reporting—because it highlights an element of the lawmaking process that these individuals are unlikely to accept as necessary or legitimate. Political sophisticates are less likely to hold this cynical view, and are more likely to base their policy support on how much they like or dislike the specific provisions contained in the legislation. Their approval or disapproval of the ACA should, therefore, not be directly affected by their beliefs about the process that created it. For these reasons, opposition to the Affordable Care Act is modeled as a function of political sophistication (measured as educational attainment), beliefs about the policy-making process, and an interaction term that multiples the two. I expect the belief that lawmakers are playing politics to have a larger impact on the policy attitudes of individuals with lower levels of education.

Support for the legislation's substantive provisions are also included in the model. The survey contained a battery of questions about those and one question about a provision proposed as part of a Republican alternative to the ACA (limits on awards in malpractice suits). For each provision, respondents were asked whether they thought it was extremely, very, somewhat, or not too important that the item be passed into law, or whether the provision should not be enacted at all. I coded responses of "extremely" and "very important" as support for the given provision. Attitudes toward five provisions were included in the model: (1) Financial assistance to help low-income families purchase insurance; (2) An expansion of Medicaid to cover more low-income families; (3) Allowing children to stay on their parents' insurance until age twenty-five; (4) Limits on future increases in Medicare payments and; (5) Limits on the amount of money that can be awarded to plaintiffs in medical malpractice suits.[3] Support for the first four provisions should decrease opposition to the ACA because they were part of the legislation. Support for the final provision should increase opposition to the ACA because it was part of an alternative proposal. The model also includes measures of ideology, partisanship, and household income.

The results of the model estimating opposition to the Affordable Care Act are displayed in table 5.8. First, notice that the coefficient on the interaction term that multiplies level of education times "playing politics" is statistically significant at a level of 95% confidence. An F-test for joint significance confirms that the interaction term and its component parts are statistically significant. As with the Clinton case, these findings show that perceptions of the policy-making process shape policy opposition. The regression results also confirm the importance of attitudes toward the substantive provisions of the Affordable Care Act and the rival GOP sponsored bills. The coefficients on all of the variables measuring support for the substantive provisions are statistically significant and their

TABLE 5.8. **Modeling Opposition to the Obama Health Reforms.**

Variable	Coefficient	Std. Error
Believes MOC Are Playing Politics	1.09*	0.53
Education	0.11	0.14
Education X Playing Politics	−0.39*	0.17
Supports Financial Assistance to Help Low-Income Families Buy Insurance	−0.76*	0.19
Supports Medicaid Expansion	−0.51*	0.18
Supports Kids on Parents' Insurance until Age 25	−0.74*	0.16
Supports Limiting Future Increases in Medicare Payments	−0.55*	0.17
Supports Limiting Malpractice Suit Damages	0.53*	0.16
Liberal	−0.41	0.24
Conservative	0.87*	0.18
Democrat	−1.13*	0.20
Republican	0.91*	0.19
Income	0.05	0.04
Constant	0.19	0.39

N = 1030
Pseudo R^2 = 0.30

Source: Kaiser Family Foundation Poll, February 2010. Results are from a logit model. *Indicates $P > 0.05$.

signs are all in the expected direction. Individuals who favor the specific elements of the ACA are less likely to oppose it while individuals who favor the alternative provisions offered by Republicans are more likely to oppose the ACA. The findings also show, not surprisingly, that Democrats are less likely to oppose the plan and that conservatives and Republicans are more likely to oppose it.

To unpack the substantive importance of the interactive term, predicted probabilities were generated for individuals with varying levels of education and are displayed in fig. 5.6. For each level of education, separate probabilities are plotted for those who believe lawmakers from both parties are playing politics (plotted in black) and for those who do not (plotted in gray). The belief that lawmakers are pursuing their political interests has the largest effect on the likelihood of opposition for individuals with the lowest level of education—those without a high school diploma. Here, individuals who believe lawmakers are playing politics are twenty-seven percentage points more likely to oppose the Affordable Care Act than are those who do not. This difference is statistically significant.[4] As individuals go up in level of educational attainment, differences in opposition based on perceptions of lawmakers' motives diminish. For individuals with a high school diploma, those with a cynical view of the process are seventeen percentage points more likely to oppose the legislation—a difference that narrowly misses the cutoff for statistical significance. For individuals with some college education or at least a four-year degree, these differences are even smaller and are not statistically significant.

These findings mirror those from the Clinton case study. In both instances, the policy opinions of individuals with the lowest levels of education were the most heavily influenced by perceptions of the policymaking process. For individuals without a high school diploma, the belief that lawmakers were playing politics increased the probability of opposition by more than twenty percentage points. This effect diminished as level of education increased. Beliefs about the lawmaking process had no discernable impact on policy opposition among individuals with at least some college. Instead, these political sophisticates were

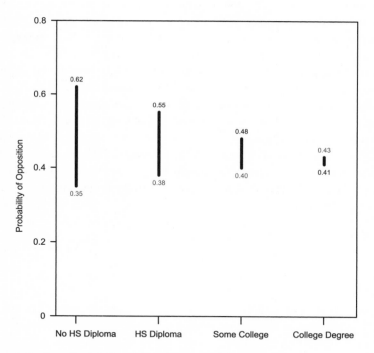

FIG. 5.6. Predicted Probability of Opposition to the Affordable Care Act.

Note: The predicted probability of opposition for individuals who do not believe lawmakers are playing politics is plotted in gray. The predicted probability of opposition for individuals who do believe lawmakers are playing politics is plotted in black. The length of the line segment indicates the degree of difference in the probability of opposition between the two groups of individuals.

more concerned with the specific provisions contained in the legislation than the process that created it.

Conclusion

For individuals who know less about how government works, perceptions of the policy-making process play an important role in shaping policy opinions. This is true even when controlling for support for the substantive elements of the policy, for partisanship, and for ideology—factors that the regression results demonstrate are also important predictors of policy opposition. Moreover, these two case studies help to demonstrate that attitudes toward policy debate, proposed laws, Congress as a whole, and the government itself are all interrelated. When partisan debate grows heated it attracts news attention, which amplifies the debate (Jacobs and Shapiro 2000). A cascade of public cynicism follows, washing over all the actors, institutions, and proposals associated with that debate. In the two cases explored here, the end result is increased disapproval of the federal government and heightened opposition to the policy under consideration. These findings suggest that at the macro level, we should find that levels of trust in government, Congressional approval, and policy support move together through time, as they are all partially influenced by the tenor of elite debate in Washington and the reflection of that debate in the news media. I explore this implication of the case studies in the concluding chapter. But, first, I examine how the news media and public respond when the policy-making process is a *bi*partisan one.

CHAPTER SIX

Exceptions that Prove the Rule

On July 26, 1990, President George H. W. Bush signed the Americans with Disabilities Act into law. The sweeping civil rights legislation prohibits discrimination on the basis of disability in a wide variety of venues, including employment, transportation, public facilities and services, public accommodations, and communications. At the time of passage, Congress estimated the new law would extend civil rights guarantees to 43 million Americans with disabilities—17% of the population. The law also had potential implications for every public transit system in the United States, every telecommunications company, and thousands of businesses.

Despite the large number of individuals and industries directly affected by the legislation, the debate over and passage of the law attracted little attention from the news media. The policy was mentioned in just sixty *New York Times* articles during the entire Congressional session in which it passed. By comparison, other important pieces of legislation enacted during the early 1990s—such as the Persian Gulf Resolution, the economic aid package for ex-Soviet republics, the ratification of NAFTA, and President Clinton's 1994 omnibus crime legislation—were mentioned in hundreds of *Times* articles. The lack of news coverage of the ADA was so striking that one scholar, Joseph Shapiro, has referred to its passage as a "stealth civil rights movement" (Shapiro 1994, 123). He argues that the lack of coverage was purposely achieved by disability rights advocates who feared that any news coverage of the legislation would reflect the stereotypes journalists held about individuals with disabilities. But many policy advocates and entrepreneurs have tried and failed to keep policy negotiations quiet for strategic reasons. Proponents of the ADA succeeded where so many others have failed for one key reason—the legislation received broad support from Republicans and Democrats alike.

Disability rights is an issue that cuts across the standard socioeconomic, racial, ethnic, and geographic divisions that stratify American society and politics. Americans with disabilities are found in all segments of society and are not traditional allies of either political party. This gives members of both parties in Congress an equal political incentive to support disability rights. At the time the ADA was debated, many members of Congress on both sides of the aisle also had personal reasons for supporting the legislation (Shapiro 1994). For instance, Senate Minority Leader Robert Dole (R-KS), an outspoken supporter of rights for the disabled, suffered an injury during WWII that left him unable to use his right arm. Representative Anthony Coelho (D-CA), who sponsored the ADA in the House, is epileptic and a long-time disability rights advocate. Senator Tom Harkin (D-IA), who introduced the legislation in the Senate, has spoken about the influence of his nephew's paraplegia and his brother's deafness on his interest in disability rights (Harkin 2012; Shapiro 1994). Senator Edward Kennedy (D-MA), another champion of disability rights, also had family members affected by disabilities. His sister, Rosemary, had a lifelong intellectual disability. His son, Ted Jr., battled bone cancer as a child and had part of his leg amputated at age twelve (Imparato 2009). Personal experiences like these helped members of Congress find common ground and forge a bipartisan alliance in support of the landmark legislation.

The bill also received strong support from President Bush. The policy's goal of integrating individuals with disabilities into the economy and workforce aligned with the president's conservative values (Berkowitz 1994). As viewed by the president, this was a policy that would put people to work rather than encouraging dependency on the state. President Bush's remarks during the signing ceremony for the ADA clearly illustrate this outlook:

> Many of our fellow citizens with disabilities are unemployed. They want to work, and they can work, and this is a tremendous pool of people. And remember, this is a tremendous pool of people who will bring to jobs diversity, loyalty, proven low turnover rate, and only one request: the chance to prove themselves. And when you add together Federal, State, local, and private funds, it costs almost $200 billion annually to support Americans with disabilities—in effect, to keep them dependent. Well, when given the oppor-

tunity to be independent, they will move proudly into the economic main-
stream of American life, and that's what this legislation is all about.

This is not to say that the legislation was entirely without opposition. Some business leaders believed that the cost of compliance with
the ADA would be too much for many companies to bear (Fasman 1989;
Scotch 2001). Additionally, some religious leaders opposed provisions in
early drafts of the bill that would have required churches to be made
fully accessible (Ball 1989). Congress carefully considered this opposition. The legislation was referred to four House committees and five sub-
committees. It was the subject of numerous public hearings, including
field hearings in Houston and Indianapolis held by the House Subcommittee on Employment Opportunities. From the introduction of the bill
to its passage, the debate and negotiations over the details of the legislation spanned fourteen months. Many exemptions, amendments, and
alterations to the legislation were agreed upon to address the concerns
raised by various interest groups and members of Congress.

The ADA was shepherded through all of these negotiations by a bipartisan coalition of legislators who were committed to the policy's success. In the end, the bill's advocates on Capitol Hill and in the White
House succeeded in rallying nearly unanimous support for the legislation. It passed in the Senate in September of 1989 with seventy-six votes
for and eight votes against. The following May the legislation passed in
the House by unanimous voice vote. The joint conference resolution that
ultimately became law was agreed to by similar margins—377 to twenty-
eight in the House and ninety-one to six in the Senate.

The ADA as Counterpoint to Contentious Legislation

The passage of the Americans with Disabilities Act is a perfect example
of "stealth democracy" (Hibbing and Theiss-Morse 2002). The level of
cooperation between high-profile political elites in Washington denied
reporters the opportunity to impose the conflict frame on the policy debate. Without two conflicting sides to the story, there was no story at
all. And so the bill was debated, passed, and enacted with little notice
from the press and even less notice from the public. Ten months after
the bill was signed into law, a Harris poll asked respondents whether any
laws had "been passed recently to give more protection to disabled peo-

ple or not" (Harris 1991).[1] Just 18% of the respondents were aware that the ADA had been enacted. Twenty percent of respondents answered that they "were not sure," and 62% answered (incorrectly) that no such law had passed. Americans who did not want "to hear about delays, debates, compromises, gridlock, egos, and agendas" seem to have gotten their wish (Hibbing and Theiss-Morse 2002, 158).

Low levels of public knowledge about the ADA are troubling from a normative perspective. But because members of the public had heard so little about the policy, the case provides an opportunity to explore how individuals who have not been subjected to the usual onslaught of conflict-focused policy reporting perceive a new law. Most of the respondents to the Harris survey learned about the legislation's passage and major provisions from subsequent poll questions rather than the news media. The poll informed respondents that the Americans with Disabilities Act had, in fact, been signed into law. Respondents were then read several provisions of the law and asked whether they supported or opposed each specific element of the bill. Respondents were also asked for their general impression of the new law, with questions like "While this new law will open up new paths of participation for disabled people, it will also in some cases be expensive to implement. Do you feel the cost will be worth it or not?"

Public support for the law's main provisions and for the law itself was very high (see fig. 6.1). Ninety-five percent of respondents supported the prohibition of employment discrimination against individuals with disabilities. Ninety-three percent supported making new public transit vehicles accessible to the disabled. And 89% believed that, overall, the cost of the new legislation would "be worth it."

Policies like the ADA that receive broad support from political elites are the exceptions that prove the rule described herein. Such policies do not lend themselves to the conflict frame, and so they attract low levels of news coverage. Without conflict-focused coverage, the policy does not become linked with the concept of governmental dysfunction in the minds of average Americans. Without this association, members of the public are less likely to view the legislation as ideologically extreme and less likely to have a negative overall impression of the bill.

I offer support for many of these assertions and show that nearly unanimous enactments receive less news coverage, on average, than do conflictual policies. I reveal that nearly unanimous enactments receive more public support, on average, than do conflictual policies. And

**Employers may not discriminate against
someone who is qualified to do a job just
because they are disabled**

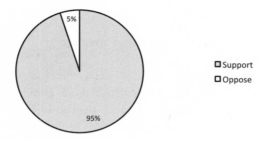

☐ Support
☐ Oppose

**New public transportation vehicles must be
made accessible to disabled people**

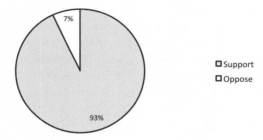

☐ Support
☐ Oppose

**While this new law will open up new paths of
participation for disabled people, it will also in
some cases be expensive to implement. Do you
feel the cost will be worth it, or not?**

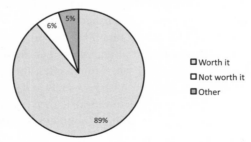

☐ Worth it
☐ Not worth it
☐ Other

FIG. 6.1. Public Support for the Americans with Disabilities Act. Source: Public Attitudes toward People with Disabilities, May 1991.

I show that conflictual policies routinely shed supporters as the legislation becomes increasingly associated with elite conflict over the course of a protracted debate.

Conflict Drives Quantity of News Coverage

Chapter 2 demonstrates that when reporters cover lawmaking, they focus on partisan conflict. Reporters also seek out contentious issues and lavish them with attention. This is done in part to attract readers and viewers and in part to fulfill the news media's role of government watchdog. When lawmakers cannot agree, the media step in to provide oversight and to inform the public about the controversy. Presumably, the public will then be the final arbiter of the dispute. Given the large quantity of legislation introduced in Congress each year, this seems like a reasonable selection criterion for determining newsworthiness. However, its use means that some very important pieces of legislation—proposals that would spend billions of dollars and affect millions of Americans— receive scant attention in the press. It also means that members of the public are unlikely to hear about lawmakers working together to solve problems—something members of the public say they want but think they don't get from their government.

To demonstrate this selection effect, I examine levels of news coverage garnered by Mayhew's (2005) important laws. David Mayhew has compiled a comprehensive list of the most important laws enacted during the postwar period. I focus on the "first sweep" laws enacted between 1981 and 2012.[2] Mayhew identified these by combing through end-of-session Congressional wrap-up reports published in the *New York Times* and the *Washington Post*. This means that all of the policies had substantive provisions that were consequential enough to get them on the radar of Capitol Hill reporters. But as I will demonstrate, the amount of coverage the laws respectively generated varies widely and is highly correlated with the degree of controversy surrounding their passage.

As a rough measure of the amount of conflict surrounding each piece of legislation, I use the final passage vote totals in the House and Senate.[3] Like the ADA, many of these important laws received bipartisan support in Congress and passed unanimously or nearly so in one or both chambers. For instance, the 1986 Goldwater-Nichols reorganization of the Defense Department, which restructured the military chain of command, passed unanimously in the Senate and with just twenty-seven votes against in the House. Similarly, the so-called Kassebaum-Kennedy Act (1996), which allowed individuals to keep their health insurance for a period after leaving a job, passed unanimously in the Senate and with just two no votes in the House. Other pieces of legislation, however, were highly contentious. President Clinton's 1993 deficit reduction plan squeaked through the House by two votes and required Vice President Al Gore's tie-breaking vote to pass in the Senate. Similarly, President George W. Bush's $350 billion tax cut (2003) was opposed by nearly all of the Democrats in the House and also required the vice president's vote for passage in the Senate.

Assessing Levels of News Coverage

To examine differences in the amount of news coverage afforded heavily contested versus nearly unanimous enactments, I first identified all of the laws that passed by either a slim majority (less than 60% in the House or 65% in the Senate) or a very wide majority (at least 90% in both houses).[4] I then ran simple key word searches of the *New York Times* digital archives in Lexis Nexis to see how many stories mentioned the legislation in the Congressional session during which it passed.

Many of the enactments focus on organizations, policies, and procedures that are not common topics of discussion outside the legislative arena. For instance, the terms "line-item veto," "unfunded mandate," and "normal trade relations" are unlikely to appear in movie reviews, crime reports, or weather forecasts. However, discussing legislation that would give the president the "line-item veto" would be nearly impossible without using that particular key term. For laws with distinctive terms like these in their titles, I simply searched for stories using the key terms during the two-year Congressional session and recorded the total number of articles returned.

For topics with less distinctive titles or titles that might be discussed outside the context of policy making, I added stipulations that the legislation's common name (such as "farm bill") be discussed within articles that also mention Congress, legislation and the like. For instance, in 2008, Congress enacted the Post-9/11 Veterans Educational Assistance Act. The legislation was commonly referred to as a new G.I. Bill because it expanded education benefits for veterans who served in post–September 11th conflicts. However, searches for "G.I. Bill" returned a mix of articles related to the new legislation and obituaries that mentioned the deceased had used the G.I. bill to finance their college education. To eliminate the latter articles from the searches, I added a stipulation that "G.I. Bill" be used in conjunction with the terms "Congress" or "legislation" or "law."

These searches cast a broad net. They identify all mentions on new laws, including discussions of the Congressional debate surrounding them, public reaction to them, discussions of their implementation, discussions of their place in the larger political agenda, and so forth. Further, the laws do not need to be the primary focus of the articles that mention them. For instance, articles mentioning the new G.I. Bill might be primarily focused on the challenges facing veterans returning home from Iraq. This type of human-interest story might only mention the new law in a single paragraph that details the veteran's plans to attend college. This low threshold for inclusion increases the likelihood that the searches will identify mentions of new laws that were passed by wide margins.

Coverage of Low- and High-Conflict Enactments

Figs. 6.2 and 6.3 show the results of the searches. On average, legislation that passed with little opposition was referenced in about seventy-seven *New York Times* articles. Some laws received far less coverage than that. The "Authorization for Use of Military Force against Terrorists," which gave the president broad, open-ended authority to use force against any individual or country involved in the September 11th attacks, was mentioned in just twenty-five articles. Only one member of Congress, Barbara Lee (D-CA), voted against the measure, which made its way through the body with little debate. The bill was signed into law on September 18, 2001, just seven days after the terrorist attacks. Because the legislation was enacted so quickly with so little debate, it attracted little attention from the press.

Other bills that received little news coverage included: the Goldwater-Nichols Act discussed above (mentioned in twenty-seven articles), President Reagan's landmark anti-drug legislation (mentioned in fifty articles), and major reforms to public housing enacted in 1998 (mentioned in just fifteen articles). In fact, roughly two-thirds of the low-conflict laws were mentioned fewer than seventy-seven times. The median number of articles is just sixty-two. The mean is inflated by coverage of a few outliers, most notably, the "Aviation and Transportation Security Act." The legislation created the Transportation Security Administration (TSA) in the wake of September 11th. It was signed into law on November 19, 2001, and continued to receive news coverage throughout the following year as new security measures were rolled out at airports nationwide.

Laws that passed by a slim margin in one or both chambers were mentioned much more often (see fig. 6.3). On average, they appeared in 407 articles per Congressional session—roughly five times more articles than the low-conflict laws. A T-test shows that the difference in means between the two groups is statistically significant. As with the low-conflict laws, however, the mean is skewed by the presence of some extreme outliers. The highly contentious Affordable Care Act (2010) passed during President Obama's first term was mentioned in 1,280 separate articles. The economic stimulus package enacted during the same session was mentioned in 2,352 articles. Without these two outliers, the mean falls to approximately 297 (still almost four times the mean of the low-conflict laws). The median number of articles is 207.

This exercise demonstrates the presence of a selection effect among policy-focused news reports. Even among laws reporters think are historic, the news media are less likely to cover legislation that is not contentious. This is true for legislation on decidedly unsexy topics like farm subsidies and water projects, as well as for legislation on topics that have greater potential to spark public interest—stiffer penalties for those convicted of narcotics possession, minimum wage increases, job discrimination statutes, the extension of the Voting Rights Act (1982), immigration reform, and aid for victims of Hurricane Katrina. Even the most extreme outlier in the low-conflict group—the post-9/11 airline security measures—failed to receive as much coverage as the average high-conflict law.

The contentious issues that received high levels of coverage also run the gamut from farm bills, transportation acts, and deficit reduction, to the ratification of NAFTA and the repeal of "Don't Ask Don't Tell." With coverage of the passage and implementation of these measures, news consumers likely got a healthy dose of exposure to the political conflict surrounding them. As demonstrated in chapters 3 and 4, exposure to such conflict then suppresses public support for the measures over time. Absent this stimulus, however, we should see higher levels of public support for government action. I compare levels of public support for nearly unanimous and contentious enactments in the next section.

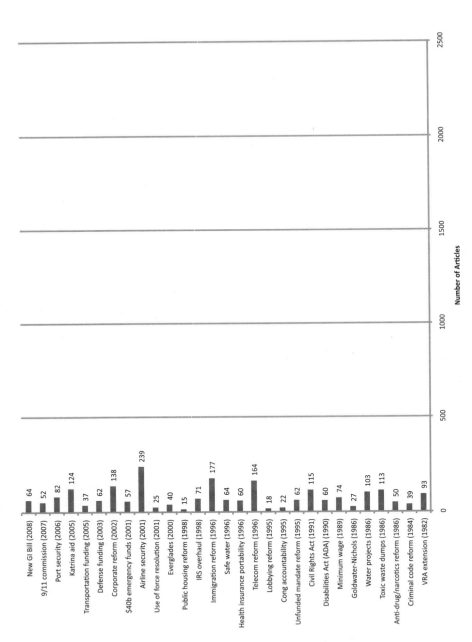

FIG. 6.2. NYT Coverage of Nearly Unanimous Enactments (1981–2012).

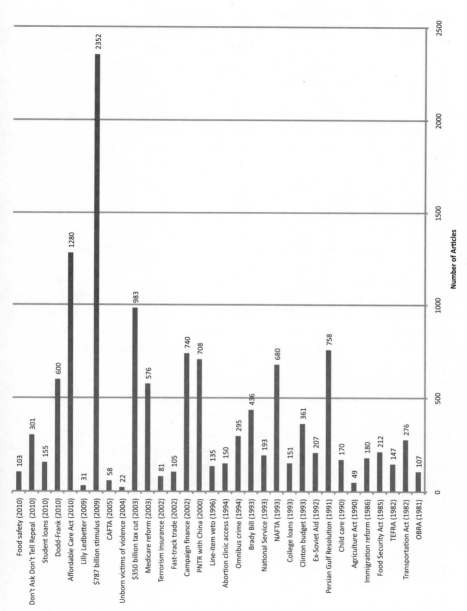

FIG. 6.3. NYT Coverage of Contentious Enactments (1981–2012).

Public Support for Low- and High-Conflict Laws

For all of the laws listed in figs. 6.2 and 6.3, I searched the Roper iPoll database for survey questions that asked whether the respondent generally favored or opposed each piece of legislation. Unfortunately, most opinion polls are commissioned by news organizations and so they tend to focus on the policies reporters believe are most newsworthy. This means bipartisan pieces of legislation are less likely to be the subject of polling questions than are contentious ones. Despite this bias in the sample I am able to construct, the exercise is still instructive. It reveals a pattern in public opinion that comports with the findings from the more scientific analyses described in chapters 3, 4, and 5.

I recorded levels of support and opposition from all survey questions that came from a poll with a representative national sample. Where more than one poll was available, I report the average amount of support and opposition to the legislation across all polls. The findings for nearly unanimous enactments are provided in fig. 6.4. The findings for contentious laws are provided in figs. 6.5 and 6.6 and are divided according to the amount of news coverage the legislation received. Attitudes toward legislation that received fewer than three hundred mentions in the *New York Times* are shown in fig. 6.5. Support for legislation with higher levels of coverage is shown in fig. 6.6.

Levels of support for nearly unanimous enactments are very high. Across the six laws for which polling data were available, the Kassebaum-Kennedy Health Insurance Portability Act received the highest level of support (88%) and unfunded mandate reform received the lowest level of public support (63%). The average level of support for the nearly unanimous enactments is 78% with a standard deviation of 8.5.

Compared to support for nearly unanimous enactments, support for high-conflict laws is lower and more variable. For the high-conflict laws mentioned in fewer than three hundred articles, the mean level of support is 54% and the standard deviation is roughly sixteen (see fig. 6.5). Here, the least popular piece of legislation was the Food Security Act of 1985. Just 31% of the public approved of the legislation according to a September 1985 *Los Angeles Times* poll. A plurality—49%—opposed it. This is not surprising given the level of intense disagreement between Congress and the Reagan Administration over the bill. The

Minimum Wage Increase

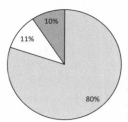

10%

11%

80%

Sources: Gallup (May 1988), ABC News/ Washington Post (March 1989)

Unfunded Mandate Reform

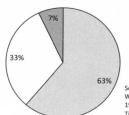

7%

33%

63%

Sources: ABC/ Washigton Post (Jan 1995, April 1995), LA Times (Jan 1995)

Congressional Accountability

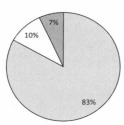

7%

10%

83%

Sources: Time/CNN/ Yankelovich (March 1995), ABC News/ Washington Post (April 1995)

Health Insurance Portability

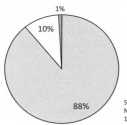

1%

10%

88%

Source: ABC News Poll (Jan 1996)

Use of Force Resolution (Afghanistan)

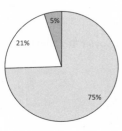

5%

21%

75%

Sources: Gallup/ CNN/ USA Today Polls (Sep 2001, Oct 2001)

Hurricane Katrina Relief Aid

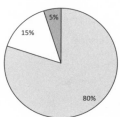

5%

15%

80%

Source: Pew News Interest Index Poll (Oct 2005)

□ Support   □ Oppose   ▣ Other

FIG. 6.4. Average Levels of Support for Low-Conflict Laws.

Note: Mean Level of Support = 78; Standard Deviation = 8.5.

CAFTA

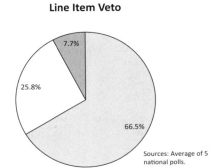

11%

50%

39%

Source: PIPA/
Knowledge Networks
Poll (June 2005)

Line Item Veto

7.7%

25.8%

66.5%

Sources: Average of 5
national polls.

Abortion Clinic Access

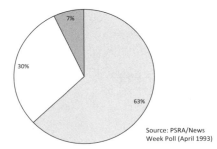

7%

30%

63%

Source: PSRA/News
Week Poll (April 1993)

Omnibus Crime Act

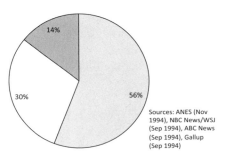

14%

30%

56%

Sources: ANES (Nov
1994), NBC News/WSJ
(Sep 1994), ABC News
(Sep 1994), Gallup
(Sep 1994)

National Service

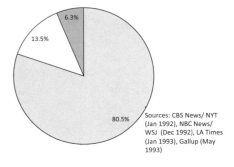

6.3%

13.5%

80.5%

Sources: CBS News/ NYT
(Jan 1992), NBC News/
WSJ (Dec 1992), LA Times
(Jan 1993), Gallup (May
1993)

Aid to Former Soviet Republics

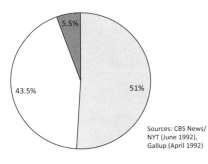

5.5%

43.5%

51%

Sources: CBS News/
NYT (June 1992),
Gallup (April 1992)

Food Security Act

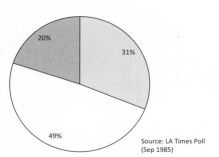

20%

31%

49%

Source: LA Times Poll
(Sep 1985)

TEFRA

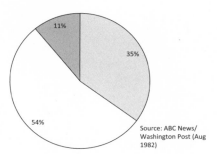

11%

35%

54%

Source: ABC News/
Washington Post (Aug
1982)

Omnibus Budget Recociliation Act (1981)

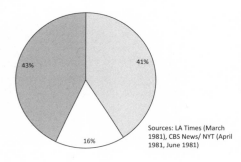

43%

41%

16%

Sources: LA Times (March
1981), CBS News/ NYT (April
1981, June 1981)

☐ Support   ☐ Oppose   ■ Other

FIG. 6.5. Average Levels of Public Support for High-Conflict Laws (fewer than 300 articles).

Note: Mean Level of Support = 54; Standard Deviation = 16.

Don't Ask Don't Tell Repeal

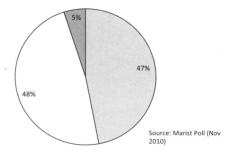

5%
47%
48%

Source: Marist Poll (Nov 2010)

Dodd-Frank

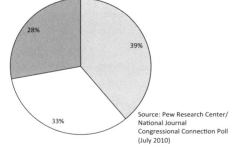

28%
39%
33%

Source: Pew Research Center/
National Journal
Congressional Connection Poll
(July 2010)

Economic Stimulus

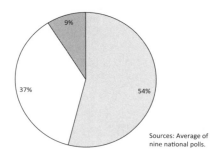

9%
54%
37%

Sources: Average of nine national polls.

Affordable Care Act

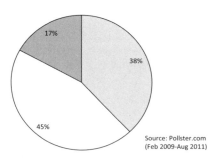

17%
38%
45%

Source: Pollster.com
(Feb 2009-Aug 2011)

Bush Tax Cuts

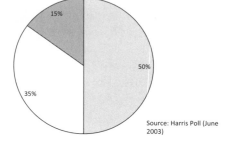

15%
50%
35%

Source: Harris Poll (June 2003)

Campaign Finance Reform

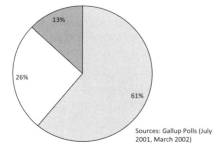

13%
26%
61%

Sources: Gallup Polls (July 2001, March 2002)

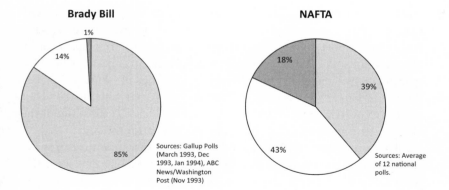

Brady Bill

1%
14%
85%

Sources: Gallup Polls
(March 1993, Dec
1993, Jan 1994), ABC
News/Washington
Post (Nov 1993)

NAFTA

18%
39%
43%

Sources: Average
of 12 national
polls.

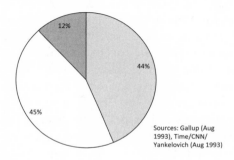

Omnibus Deficit Reduction Act (1993)

12%
44%
45%

Sources: Gallup (Aug
1993), Time/CNN/
Yankelovich (Aug 1993)

☐ Support ☐ Oppose ■ Other

FIG. 6.6. Average Levels of Public Support for High-Conflict Laws (at least 300 articles).

Note: Mean Level of Support = 50.8; Standard Deviation = 14.9.

conflict spanned nearly two years and centered on provisions related to commodity price supports, loan guarantees for farmers, export subsidies, and import quotas. The disagreement was so intractable that in March of 1985, President Reagan vetoed the legislative package initially sent to him by Congress. The veto prompted groups of farmers to picket the White House (de Lama and Donosky 1985), but without the votes needed to override the veto, the legislation was dead. A substitute farm bill was, therefore, introduced in Congress days after the veto. The new legislation ultimately included a number of conservation measures including the "Swampbuster" and "Sodbuster" provisions that were the subject of public lobbying campaigns by groups such as the Audubon Society and the Sierra Club (Malone 1986). Debate over the substitute bill dragged on for eight months before the president signed the legislation into law on December 23rd, 1985.

The policy that received the highest level of public support by far (80.5%) was Bill Clinton's 1993 National and Community Service Trust Act. The legislation created AmeriCorps, a program that offers young people money toward their college education in exchange for community service. While the final passage vote totals place the legislation in the "contentious" category, the program received modest bipartisan support in both chambers. In the House, there were nineteen Republicans among the bill's 221 cosponsors. In the Senate, the final conference report received support from Republicans John Chafee, David Durenberger, Mark Hatfield, James Jeffords, Arlen Specter, and Ted Stevens. This bipartisanship helped the bill move through the legislative process quickly. President Clinton signed the program into law less than five months after it was introduced in Congress. The speedy passage, the bipartisan support, and the substance of the law itself all likely contributed to its public popularity.

These two cases exemplify the types of policies that are likely to receive high and low levels of public approval. Policies that attract bipartisan support and make their way through the legislative process quickly (like the National Community Service Trust Act), will be viewed more favorably by the public. Policies that generate heated debate over the course of many months or years (like the 1985 Farm Bill), will receive lower levels of support. This pattern is also observed for the contentious enactments that received higher levels of news coverage.

The average level of support for the contentious laws that were mentioned in at least three hundred news articles is 50.8% with a median of 48.5% and standard deviation of 14.9 (see fig. 6.6). Support was lowest for the 2010 Affordable Care Act, which I have discussed at length previously. Just 39% of the public supported the plan and 45% opposed it. The 2010 Dodd-Frank financial services regulation package was similarly unpopular (it was favored by 39% of the public), as was the 1993 free trade treaty, NAFTA (also favored by 39% of the public).

An Important Outlier: The Brady Bill

The contentious policy with the highest level of public support (85%) was the 1993 Brady Bill. The measure sought to impose a one-week waiting period on the sale of firearms so that background checks could be performed on perspective purchasers before sales were finalized. The legislation was modeled after similar state laws and was framed by proponents as a policy response to the attempted assassination of President Reagan in 1981. Naming the bill after Jim Brady, President Reagan's press secretary who was also wounded in the shooting, clearly linked the legislation to the assassination attempt. This framing helped to establish the public popularity of the plan and also helped to attract modest bipartisan support for the proposal (including an endorsement from President Reagan). Despite this public support, however, the policy faced vehement opposition from gun rights advocates.

The Brady Bill was first introduced in 1987 and was subsequently reintroduced in each Congressional session until its passage. Opposition to the measure came primarily from the National Rifle Association, which lobbied aggressively and successfully against it during the 100th, 101st, and 102nd Congresses. One of the key strategies used by the group and its allies in Congress was to attach the gun control measure to a comprehensive crime bill (Aborn 1994). This gave members of Congress who opposed the popular policy political cover—they could vote against the multifaceted crime legislation without directly opposing gun control.

Recognizing the potency of this tactic, gun control supporters began calling for a stand-alone Brady Bill in the fall of 1992 (Aborn 1994). Advocates believed that separating the measure from the broader discussion of crime prevention would heighten the salience of the gun control debate and expose the true motives of lawmakers who had repeatedly voted down the crime bill. The pressure of public opinion would then (ostensibly) force some of the plan's opponents to acquiesce. Opinion polls showed this strategy had the potential for success. Eighty-eight percent of those surveyed by Gallup in March of 1993 stated support for the stand-alone Brady Bill.

On the campaign trail in 1992, then Governor Bill Clinton voiced his support for the stand-alone bill, which he reaffirmed in his first State of the Union Address after assuming the presidency. With support from the White House and the public behind it, proponents in Congress wasted no time in introducing the legislation. Rep. Charles Schumer (D-NY) and Senator Howard Metzenbaum (D-OH) introduced the Brady Bill in their respective chambers in February of 1993. The legislation quickly gained numerous cosponsors in the House (including seventeen Republicans) and was referred to committee.

Progress on the legislation then stalled. Proponents in the Senate were unable to attain the sixty votes needed to invoke cloture and bring the bill to a vote. With supporters and detractors unable to find a compromise that satisfied both sides, some in the news media began to pronounce the bill dead (*Los Angeles Times* 1993). Yet public support for the legislation remained high. A November 1993 ABC News Poll showed that 84% of the public approved of the policy. Feeling pressure from the public, the bill's opponents in the Senate finally lifted their objections and allowed the measure to come to a vote. The bill passed the Senate by a margin of sixty-three to thirty-six (which included sixteen Republican votes in favor of the measure) and the House by a margin of 238 to 189. The two slightly different versions of the legislation were then sent to the conference committee and the conference report was approved in short order by both chambers. President Clinton signed the bill into law on November 30, 1993. A year-end poll conducted by Gallup found that 79% of Americans supported the measure at the conclusion of the debate (Gallup 1991).

The passage of the Brady Bill is ultimately the story of politicians yielding to public pressure. Popular support for the legislation was so high that members of Congress simply could not hold out their opposition in the face of it. But this is also the story of a political strategy that overcame the usual challenges associated with the conflict frame—the uncoupling of problems and solutions and the lack of attention to policy substance. This piece of legislation was clearly and directly linked to the problem it was meant to solve. It was meant to prevent people like John Hinckley, Jr., from getting their hands on a weapon and shooting the president, his press secretary, a police officer, and a secret service agent. Because the law bore the name of Reagan's wounded press secretary and because Jim Brady's wife, Sarah, was one of the bill's chief public advocates, this linkage between problem and solution could not be obscured. Further, by pressing for a stand-alone piece of legislation—a concise bill with provisions that were easy for the public to understand— the measure's advocates ensured that members of the public would grasp how the bill would achieve its goal of preventing gun violence. This transparency left little room for opponents to question the motives of the bill's backers. Despite the political debate surrounding the legislation, members of the public did not view the bill as one drafted to score political points. They understood that it had been drafted because the president had been shot and the legislation sought to prevent that from happening again. The moderate level of bipartisan support the bill garnered reaffirmed this assessment.

As demonstrated by figs. 6.5 and 6.6, few contested policies receive levels of support approaching that of the Brady Bill. Only the National Community Service Trust Act (discussed above) comes close. Even with these extreme outliers, the overall average level of support for contentious laws is roughly 52%. This stands in contrast to the high levels of support garnered by nearly unanimous enactments—78% on average. Moreover, these averages mask differences in levels of support for contentious policies over time. Support for high-conflict bills often diminishes as the debate extends over a period of months or years and the public hears more and more about the controversy. The final level of support for a hotly debated policy may be well below its mean level of support.

Support for High-Conflict Laws over Time

For many of the high-conflict enactments, multiple polls were fielded that gauged public support for the legislation over a period of several months. Where such data are available and the questions asked are similarly worded, I am able to examine support and opposition to the legislation over time.[5] Fig. 6.7 displays plots of support and opposition for each of these cases.

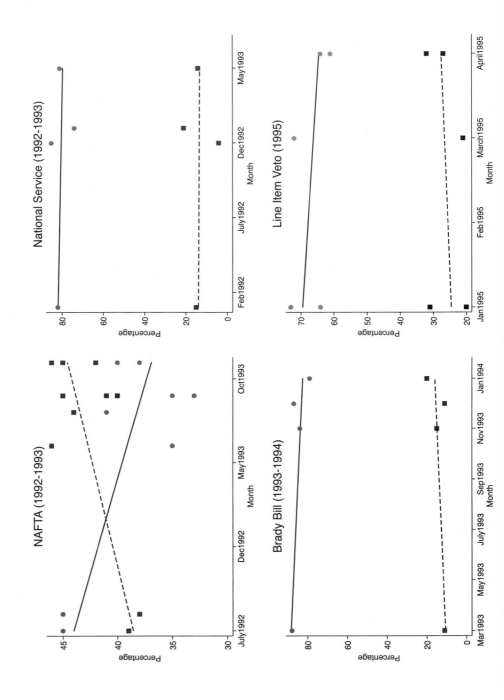

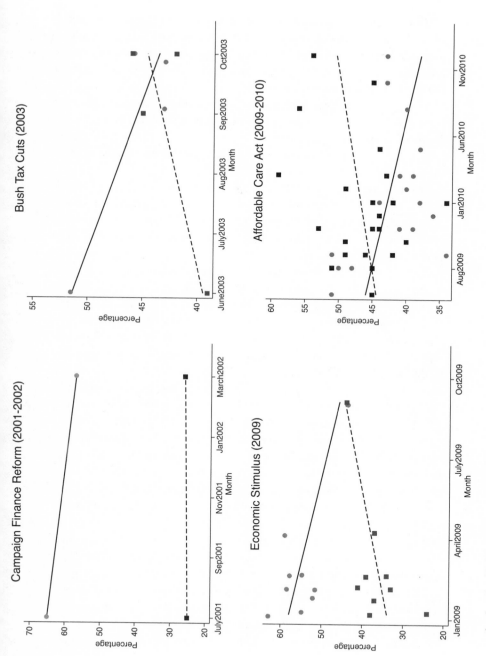

FIG. 6.7. Levels of Public Support over Time.

Support clearly decreases over time for five of the eight policies for which data are available. These policies are: NAFTA, campaign finance reform, the Bush tax cuts, the 2009 economic stimulus, and the Affordable Care Act. This group includes laws with relatively high initial levels of support (like campaign finance reform, which started with 65% approval) and laws with relatively low initial levels of support (like NAFTA, which had 45% support in the earliest available poll). The size of the decrease in support ranges from eight percentage points in the case of campaign finance reform to roughly twelve percentage points in the case of the 2009 economic stimulus.

Support for the Brady Bill and the line item veto is nearly flat, dipping just a few points over the period for which polls are available. Support for Clinton's National Service Act does not change over time. I find no instances in which a contentious law gained support over the course of the debate.

This evidence is merely suggestive because of the use of a convenience sample, but it points to the same conclusion as do the results of the controlled experiments presented in chapter 3, the gay marriage case study given in chapter 4, and the health care case studies proffered in chapter 5. The public responds negatively to heated, protracted policy debate. This means that proponents of new policies that are challenged in the public forum face a huge obstacle. Not only will the new plan almost always fail to gain supporters over the course of a well-publicized debate, but it will likely shed supporters and amass opponents over time. Savvy policy advocates may, therefore, attempt to keep the debate surrounding their pet legislation out of the press to avoid this attrition of support. Few will succeed, however. Reporters are able to smell blood in the political waters and are attracted to its scent. As demonstrated here, conflict is an important criterion of newsworthiness and its presence significantly increases the odds that a bill will receive media attention.

Conversely, lawmakers who wish to highlight their role in the passage of important bipartisan legislation may have trouble garnering media coverage. When legislators are in agreement, journalists believe there is less need for oversight and that there will be less interest from the public. I will not presume to know whether these beliefs are based in fact. They may well be. But I will suggest that this selection effect leaves members of the public with a skewed perception of their government. Citizens hear continuously about the instances in which lawmakers seem to be working against one another and hear little about the important instances in which lawmakers are working together for the good of the country. Given this lopsided coverage of Washington, we should not be surprised to learn that Americans are disgusted with and distrustful of their government.

CHAPTER SEVEN

Conclusion

Democracy demands an informed public and the press—the fourth branch of our government—is charged with the daunting task of doing the informing. Each day, reporters sift through, digest, and condense huge amounts of political information into a few minutes of nightly TV news or a handful of column inches. The stories they produce are meant to give citizens the information they need to evaluate their elected officials. They are also designed to engage an audience that is only mildly interested in politics and has innumerable options for both news and entertainment.

To meet this dual goal of informing and engaging, journalists look for conflict. As demonstrated in the last chapter, members of the press devote far more attention to divisive issues than unifying ones. They also structure their reports in ways that emphasize disagreements between political elites. This narrative structure enlivens stories about lawmaking and attracts news consumers. It also helps reporters fulfill their watchdog role. When lawmakers cannot agree, journalists step in to provide oversight and to inform the public about the controversy. By presenting both sides of the debate to the public, the press gives the people the information it needs to serve as the final arbiter of the dispute. This makes conflict a decisive criterion of newsworthiness. Conversely, when conflict is not present, reporters are far less likely to cover elite actions.

These standards of newsworthiness seem reasonable, but I have demonstrated the profound impact the news medias' focus on conflict—and inattention to bipartisanship—has on public opinion. Because of the selection criterion journalists employ, Americans hear very little about the numerous instances of compromise and bipartisanship that lawmakers routinely display on the Hill. They also hear little about policies like the Americans with Disabilities Act that receive strong support from elites and citizens alike. Instead, they learn from the news media about elected officials fighting, battling, and bickering over pieces of contentious legislation.

When these battles explode in the national headlines, journalists' use of the conflict frame focuses public attention on the political ramifications of the dispute. The content analysis provided in chapter 2 demonstrates that reports about lawmaking almost always provide information about who is winning, who is losing, what parliamentary and political tactics are being employed, or how the debate will impact approval ratings and election outcomes. Substantive information about the content of major reform legislation—which is often viewed positively by large segments of the public—is provided within this overarching narrative of political conflict. Few reports focus on how the proposed legislation will resolve the problem it is meant to address. As a result, the public views the debate as a sign that lawmakers are pursing political goals rather than public ones. In short, many Americans view heated debate as a sign of misplaced priorities and a dysfunctional government.

The experimental results outlined in chapter 3 illustrate this dynamic. Exposure to conflict increased the share of student participants who believed the policy-making process was broken by twenty-two percentage points. This finding is striking and it comports with the observational data regarding attitudes toward the government during the Clinton and Obama health care debates. During both of those contentious debates, public impressions of the government soured. By the end of the Clinton debate in the fall of 1994, enthusiasm for government was down by half (to 2%), satisfaction with government was down three points (to 26%), and anger was up five points (to 21%). The share of the public that believed debate in Congress stemmed from honest disagreement about policy (as opposed to a desire to score political points) fell from 14% to 9% over the course of the debate.

Members of the public were similarly cynical during the debate over "Obamacare." Nearly three-quarters of respondents surveyed at the height of the debate stated it demonstrated that "our policymaking process is broken," rather than working as intended (Kaiser 2010a). Less than a quarter of respondents (24%) believed members of both parties in Congress were motivated by fundamental disagreements about policy rather than politics.

The negative reactions to political debate documented here reaffirm the findings of other scholars, like Capella and Jamieson (1996). But the evidence I provided in chapters 3 through 6 goes beyond what was already known about the link between debate and public cynicism by demonstrating how exposure to partisan conflict also shapes public policy opinion. The mere association of a policy with intense conflict results in decreased support for that policy. Through both a direct and an indirect mechanism, exposure to political conflict dampens support for policy reform—even when the proposed law contains provisions that have broad public support. Hotly debated policies seem ideologically extreme and politically motivated to the American people. As shown in chapters 3, 4, and 5, both of these beliefs dampen support and increase opposition to proposed legislation. The longer and more intense the debate, the more dramatic the public backlash. As demonstrated in chapter 6, new plans at the center of well-publicized debates typically shed supporters and amass opponents over time.

This decline in support can affect a policy's chance of passage and the degree to which it is successfully implemented if enacted. As demonstrated by Erik Patashnik (2008) in *Reforms at Risk*, the political will for reform sometimes stalls after new policies are signed into law. This can prevent reforms from being fully implemented and sometimes leads to the passage of successive laws designed to reverse the initial reforms. The history of the Affordable Care Act offers a clear example of this type of backsliding. The law was enacted during President Obama's first term, during which he enjoyed Democratic majorities in both Houses of Congress. But the political winds that swept the Democrats into office had shifted by the fall of 2010. The midterm elections gave Republicans control of the House and additional seats in the Senate—a reversal of fortune that the president described as a "shellacking" (Branigin 2010). Just as Patashnik (2008) anticipates, "reform coalitions [held] power only momentarily" (155). The new Republican majority in the House quickly set about trying to repeal, defund, and block the implementation of the president's landmark health care law. Growing public antipathy for the law (especially among conservatives) fueled their resolve. Only the slim Democratic majority in the Senate and the threat of the president's veto pen kept the law from being dismantled months after it was enacted. Undaunted, Congressional Republicans continued to challenge the law throughout Obama's presidency and to use promises of repeal as a conservative rallying cry. The attrition of support the plan suffered, due in part to its portrayal in the media, had long-lasting consequences for the president's signature law.

Macro-Level Implications

When taken together, these findings indicate that attitudes toward policy debate, toward proposed laws, toward policymakers, and toward the government itself are all interrelated. When partisan debate grows heated it attracts news attention, which amplifies the debate. A cascade of public cynicism then follows in response, washing over all the actors, institutions, and proposals associated with it. The study of trust in and support for the government must, therefore, be integrated into the study of policy approval and vice versa. To some degree, both are responsive to the same stimuli—the tenor of elite debate—and they feedback on and reinforce one another.

Approval of Congress and the president is also a part of this self-reinforcing system. Involvement in a politically motivated policy spat tarnishes the public's view of these actors. The two health care case studies described above and in chapter 5 illustrate this dynamic. As public support for the Administration's reform policies diminished over the course of the respective debates, so too did approval of Congress and the government as a whole. Approval of the president's job performance also suffered (see fig. 7.1). President Clinton began his first term with an approval rating of nearly 60%, only to see it topple to 40% by the end of his second year. President Obama began his first term with an approval rating near 70%, which quickly eroded to approximately 50% by the time he signed the Affordable Care Act into law in March of 2010. President Obama's job approval on health care, specifically, fell from 51% to 42% during the height of the debate—the spring and summer of 2009 (Pew 2009e).

Numerous factors influence levels of presidential approval, of course. Some of these, like the state of the economy, foreign conflicts, and personal scandal are briefly touched on in chapter 5. I do not want to overstate the influence of any single factor, but I will suggest that how long the presidential honeymoon lasts depends in part on how soon and how forcefully the president begins to push for major reform—and how vocally the opposition party denounces it. Presidents who champion

President Clinton

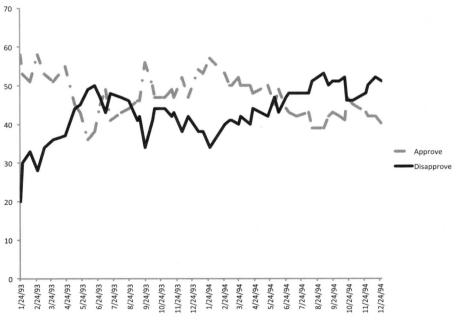

President Obama

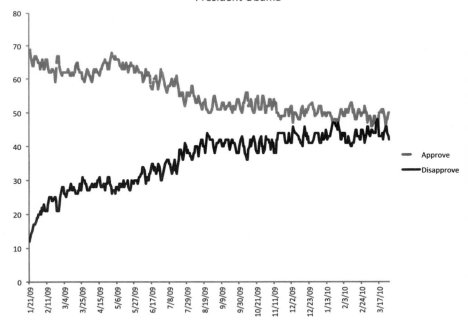

FIG. 7.1. Presidential Job Approval.

Source: The American Presidency Project.

heavily debated policies can expect to see their approval ratings fall, just as they can expect to see support for their legislation decrease, and public cynicism climb.

For this reason, presidents and lawmakers in the majority party are "damned if they do and damned if they don't." These actors are charged with governing. If they fail to act on issues of societal concern, it will surely generate public criticism. But just as surely, proposing solutions that generate controversy will also produce public disapproval. This is why authors like Jacobs and Shapiro (2000) find that policy proponents carefully craft positive messages designed to attract public support. They know that if the dominant storyline is one about the conflict-laden process of lawmaking, it will be to the advantage of policy opponents. But supporters of reform are only rarely able to keep public attention focused on a policy's problem-solving potential.

As outlined in chapter 6, the Brady Bill was one such reform that beat the odds—public support for it never waivered despite a long fight between the bill's supporters and the NRA. But the gun control measure had several factors in its favor that are difficult to replicate. It was proposed in the wake of a national tragedy (the attempted assassination of President Reagan) and was clearly aimed at preventing another such tragedy from happening in the future. Because the law bore the name of Reagan's wounded press secretary and because Jim Brady's wife, Sarah, was one of the bill's chief public advocates, this linkage between problem and solution could not be obscured. The legislation also had modest bipartisan support in Congress and endorsements from Presidents Clinton and Reagan.

Few contested policies have such strong odds in their favor. More often, members of the minority party are able to exploit the medias' infatuation with conflict to their advantage by frequently and fervently accusing the majority party of playing politics, manipulating parliamentary rules, strong-arming their own members, and ramming through ideologically extreme legislation. When such details of the "ugly" policy-making process dominate public dialogue, even policies that seem to give Americans exactly what they want—more education funding, more affordable health care, lower taxes, and so on—can backfire on their proponents. Support for the status quo is reinforced in these instances, and so is the minority party's commitment to conflict. These self-reinforcing dynamics keep Washington locked in a negative feedback loop.

Normative Implications and Proposed Solutions

These findings have troubling normative implications. This book's central finding is that Americans frequently reject policies they like because they misunderstand the nature of political debate. The belief that *all* conflict and debate are signs of dysfunction in government is misguided. In a free society made up of individuals with a multitude of values, viewpoints, and preferences, conflict over the best course of action for the nation is inevitable. As so eloquently put by James Madison, "Liberty is to faction what air is to fire." The only way to eliminate conflict is to deny citizens free expression or to give "to every citizen the same opinions, the same passions, and the same interests" (Madison, Federalist Paper no. 10).

Like average citizens, members of Congress also have differing opinions, passions, and interests—and across the two parties those opinions are shaped by fundamentally different worldviews. The parties are divided by opposing beliefs about the government's proper role in society. Where one believes a small federal government should craft public policy that promotes self-reliance, the other believes a robust federal government should prioritize a commitment to social responsibility. These very real differences in deeply held core values underscore political conflict in America. Public debate can provide an opportunity to weigh the merits and demerits of both worldviews and the policies designed to advance them. But most Americans don't see things that way.

Politicians and journalists have turned debate into a dirty word by obscuring its legitimate function in a democracy. By overemphasizing the policy-making process and the political ramifications of reform plans— and by outright denouncing policy debate as an impediment to problem solving—these elites have created a sort of self-fulfilling prophecy. Debate *can* be an impediment to problem solving when it is used as a rhetorical weapon designed to kill policy proposals rather than as a tool to try and better them.

This is only possible because journalists indulge the theatrics and outlandish claims made by Capitol Hill's most telegenic and most extreme characters. Few reporters believe it is their job to go "beyond the statements of the contending sides to the hard facts of a political dispute" (Patterson 2007, 29). So journalists report what politicians are eager to give them—carefully worded attacks of the motives and methods used by policy advocates to promote their agendas. From one president to the next, from one bill to the next, the arguments from the opposition party are the same and so are the headlines: The legislation is being rammed through. The parties are locked in a standoff. The ideological proposal goes too far. The president has threatened to veto.

Headlines about bipartisan efforts at cooperation are largely absent.

This type of reporting is not unbiased. It is exactly the type of news coverage policy proponents fear and policy opponents hope to generate. The politicians behind these headlines are playing on the public's mis- understanding of and misgivings about a policy-making process that is often adversarial. When reporters highlight these claims and make po- litical conflict the dominant frame in their reporting, they are advan- taging the status quo. Such reports stoke public anxiety, heighten pub- lic cynicism, and obscure the legitimate role of debate in the lawmaking process. Moreover, members of the press are skewing public perceptions of the government by deemphasizing instances of cooperation on Capi- tol Hill. They do this despite knowing that the American public is sick of bad news. All the nightly network newscasts have attempted to slake viewers' desires for more feel good news by creating regular segments devoted to it. These segments highlight the good works of philanthropic organizations, they herald the ingenuity of small communities, and they celebrate individuals who have overcome adversity. But there seems to be an unwritten rule that the news media must not praise the accom- plishments of our federal government or its elected leaders.

This blind spot in journalists' coverage makes it difficult for politi- cians to claim and receive credit for good deeds—like offering innova- tive solutions, protecting their constituents, conserving resources, build- ing coalitions, and reaching across the aisle. Instead, it is much easier for politicians to gain publicity and take credit for blocking legislation and tearing down their opponents. If this reward structure were altered, however—if politicians could get as much press for doing good as they can for lashing out at one another—the self-reinforcing incentives that allow politicians to wield partisan conflict as a weapon would begin to erode.

Journalists should reconsider their notions of balanced coverage and expand them to make way for more substantive coverage of proposed legislation, more positive reports about the government *when such cov- erage is warranted*, more coverage of bipartisan efforts, and more fact checking. Public affairs reporters should also strive to better connect information about policy provisions to the problems they are designed to ameliorate. This would allow journalists to give Americans more of what they say they want from the news media—information about the likely effects of proposed legislation on people like themselves. It might also help Americans better understand the differences between various proposals that sometimes underscore genuine disagreement.

Finally, reporters should more carefully evaluate the veracity of politicians' claims about the extreme nature of policy proposals and the legislative process because such claims have the ability to systematically increase public cynicism and decrease public policy support. When lawmakers argue that the public will is being ignored, claim that a government take-over is afoot, describe legislation as a right-wing conspiracy, or assert that the policy-making process is broken, reporters should investigate these serious accusations. They should consider it part of their "watch-dog" role to suss out whether lawmakers are crying wolf, to hold them accountable when they are, and to spotlight their concerns when they are not. This would give news consumers greater insight into the mixture of motives—both political and genuine—that shape policy debate.

Input from nonpartisan experts should be drawn on more frequently to help make these determinations. Expert sources can provide journalists with the information needed to put current debates into historical perspective, to evaluate the potential merits and demerits of competing proposals, and to analyze legal precedents. They can also provide background information on parliamentary rules, summarize the content and ideological thrust of complex legislation, and provide nuanced insight into public preferences. With this type of input, journalists can debunk claims that the political process is broken when in fact it is not.

Educators also have a role to play in changing the incentive structure that promotes attention to conflict. Politicians' attempts at shaping public opinion by heightening conflict are successful, in part, because many Americans do not understand the legitimate role that debate can and should play in a democracy. Students from grade school to graduate school need to get the message that, while debate sometimes serves political interests, it is a vital component of a democratic society. There is no one best solution to any of the problems we face as a nation. Choosing between policy options always involves considering one's values, establishing priorities, making tradeoffs and compromises, calculating future benefits and costs—and yes, considering the political ramifications of each alternative. This process should unfold in full view of the public so that citizens can evaluate for themselves the work their government is doing. The policy-making process may generate conflict. It may drag on for months. It may be shaped by arcane parliamentary procedures. It may spawn alternative proposals and activate interest groups. It may be messy and complex—because that is exactly the way the Founders designed it.

We should teach our students to expect political debate and to view it as part of a functioning democracy. If we inoculate them against the idea that debate always signifies dysfunction in the government, its association with a policy proposal will no longer mean an automatic black mark against the legislation. If our strides are coupled with an increase in substance-focused reporting, over time we should see the policies that give Americans what they want enjoy higher levels of public support, a greater likelihood of passage, and a better shot at successful implementation.

Appendices

Creating Keywords for News Searches

To create the news database needed for the study, I conducted keyword searches of the *New York Times* in Lexis Nexis. Because the theory tested pertains to national events and news coverage, articles from particular sections or "desks" of the *Times* that generate editorials, foreign news, sports, local news, etc., were omitted. Those desks are metropolitan, editorial, foreign, weekly, book review, arts and leisure, travel, sports, and society.

The search terms were developed through an iterative process. An initial set of search terms for each category was developed using the Policy Agendas codebook as a guide. The Agendas coding scheme systematically categorizes the issues that come before Congress into nineteen major topics and 229 subtopics. The Agendas codebook, therefore, describes a wide range of policies and programs that fall into specific issue areas, like health, education, and poverty assistance.[1] These descriptions provided a useful starting point for the keywords I developed. I augmented these mostly policy-focused keywords with terms that described the underlying societal problems.

I ran searches using the initial keywords and read through a sample of the stories returned. I then iteratively revised the search terms until at least 90% of the articles returned by them were "true hits"—meaning the search terms were used in the intended context.[2] Sensitivity studies were also conducted to ensure the search results were not driven by the inclusion of a single key term. Iteratively removing one of the terms contained within each set of keywords and rerunning the searches achieved this. The keywords were approved when the annual number of articles returned with and without each individual term was highly correlated (with a correlation coefficient of at least .85). For instance, the health keywords include the term "Medicare." To ensure that articles about this particular policy did not dominate the health database, I removed the word "Medicare" from the set of keywords and ran the search again. I then compared the annual number of articles returned with and without the inclusion of "Medicare." Because the two searches were highly correlated with one another, I felt confident that the results were not driven by a single key term. After the keywords were vetted in this manner, the full text of all the articles returned by these searches was downloaded and imported into an Access database.[3]

Codebook for Content Analysis

Coding Procedures

Research assistants worked with the author to complete the initial round of coding in which the "policy" and "problem" codes were applied. Before working with virgin data, all coders worked with a training dataset that had been coded by the author. The research assistants (who could not see the author's codes) independently coded the training dataset in small batches of approximately fifty articles at a time. At the end of each batch, their codes were compared to those of the author. Any discrepancies in codes were addressed and the coding rules described herein were clarified to facilitate more uniform and accurate coding. Once the coders reached a level of 85% agreement with the author's codes, they were assigned virgin text. To allow for an assessment of inter-coder reliability, a 25% sample of virgin text was independently coded by two coders. The level of inter-coder reliability was approximately 89%.

Only the articles that received either the "policy" or the "problem" code were eligible for further coding. The conflict, spending, substance, and human-interest codes described herein were applied by the author in a second round of coding.

General Guidelines for the Application of the Policy-Focus Code

To receive the policy-focus code, at least 50% of the article should pertain to a policy initiative in Congress related to domestic policy in the areas of health, education, or welfare. This includes descriptions of federal legislation (which is being drafted, has been proposed, or has recently

passed), the potential effects of that legislation, the legality of such legislation, or the debate, opinions, or political compromises surrounding the
legislation. These articles generally mention actors such as the president,
members of Congress, congressional groups (like congressional Democrats or congressional Republicans) and congressional leaders (like the
Speaker of the House, House/Senate Minority/Majority leader, etc.).

- Letters to the editor, op-eds, and other opinion pieces should not receive this
  code.
- These articles MUST have a legislative component. If an administrative
  agency or the Supreme Court is the main actor and the article does not discuss congressional action or a presidential policy initiative, the article cannot
  be coded as POLICY.
- If the article centers on problems with existing health, education, or welfare policies or programs, the article should be coded as "problem-focused"
  rather than "policy-focused." For example, an article focused on the fact that
  current welfare payments are not sufficient to meet the needs of low-income
  families should receive the "problem" code. (But note that articles can be
  double coded as both policy- and problem-focused if equal weight is given
  to policy solutions and the societal problems those policies are designed to
  address.)
- Articles about state and local policies should not receive this code.

General Guidelines for the Application of
the Problem-Focus Code

Here, health, education and welfare are discussed outside the context
of government action and the article focuses on a societal problem (like
increasing rates of diabetes, falling test scores, or an increasing poverty
rate).

- If the problem described is a fluke (meaning it affects one person, one town,
  or one business but has no implications for a larger segment of society), it
  should NOT receive this code. EXAMPLE: The health care dataset contains an article about a pet store where a kitten was discovered to have rabies. Hundreds of people came in contact with the kitten before it was known
  to be infected and all of those people required rabies shots. This was a fluke

and was not representative of a larger problem with exposure to rabies in pet stores. This article should not receive the "societal problem" code.

- Most articles about legislation being considered will discuss the possible ill effects of the policy (i.e., the article will discuss the possibility of future problems that *could* result from the passage of the bill). This type of discussion should NOT be given the "societal problem" code. Only descriptions of existing societal problems warrant the problem code.
- Letters to the editor, op-ed, or other opinion pieces should not be given this code.

Topic-Specific Codes

Health

Articles are eligible for the "health policy" and "health problem" codes if the main focus is domestic health or health care, meaning the American health care system; the cost of health care in the US; the state of health care in the US; threats to public health; access to health care; health policy; innovations in medicine; or the cause, effects, or treatment of a particular disease/disorder.

- Note, this category does not include business-focused articles about the price of Kaiser stock, the sale or merging of health care companies, etc., *unless* the article goes on to discuss the ways the business transaction will affect the cost or quality of health care, access to health coverage, the price of prescription drugs, etc.
- A note about abortion. Articles about abortion should only be coded as health if abortion is discussed in the context of health (as part of a plan to reform health care, for example). If abortion is mentioned as a stand-alone issue (such as legislation requiring parents to be notified if a minor seeks an abortion), it should *not* be coded as health.
- The health policy code is designed to loosely map on with Policy Agendas Topic Code 301: comprehensive health care reform. Examples of legislation considered "health policy": comprehensive health care reform; Medicare reform/funding; Medicaid reform/funding; regulation of health insurance; the regulation, coverage, and cost of prescription drugs and medical devices; the Children's Health Insurance Program (CHIP); the regulation of state health care reform; initiatives in women's health; initiatives in rural health.

- The health problem code applies to articles where the main focus (at least 50%) is related to issues such as lack of accessible health care, the rising prevalence of particular diseases/disorders, risks to public health, the high cost of health care, problems funding Medicare or Medicaid, lack of medical specialists or personnel, understaffing in hospitals, Medicare fraud, or the inadequacy or ill effects of existing health policies.

Welfare

The main focus of the article is social welfare, meaning the American social safety net in general; appropriations and budget requests for means tested programs; the Administration's welfare reform proposals; the effectiveness of federal and state welfare/public assistance programs; the problems of poverty, hunger and homelessness; the needs of low-income families and children; discussions of the poverty rate; the effects of budget cuts on low-income individuals and families; mandatory work and training programs for welfare recipients.

- The "welfare policy" code is designed to loosely map on with Policy Agendas Topic Codes 1301 (Food Stamps, Food Assistance, and Nutrition Monitoring Programs) and 1302 (Poverty and Assistance for Low-Income Families). Legislation related to means-tested programs is considered "welfare policy." This primarily includes Aid to Families with Dependent Children (AFDC); Temporary Assistance to Needy Families (TANF); Personal Responsibility and Work Opportunity Reconciliation Act (PRWORA); Earned Income Tax Credit (EITC) and other tax credits for low-income people; HHS energy assistance programs; Economic Opportunity Act antipoverty programs; child welfare issues associated with the Social Security Act; food stamps; free and reduced price school lunch programs; Medicaid; subsidized housing; and WIC.
  - Social programs that are not explicitly aimed at aiding the impoverished (such as universal health care plans, Medicare, Social Security) should *not* automatically receive the welfare code. Only when articles about these programs go on to explicitly describe how the program will affect poverty or the welfare of low-income/impoverished people should the article be given the "welfare" code.
- The "welfare problem" code applies to articles where the main focus relates to issues such as poverty, hunger, homelessness, the needs/ problems of low-

income families, the effects of the high cost of living or a slow economy on low-income/working class families, problems funding existing welfare programs, abuse of the social safety net (i.e., articles about "welfare queens" who won't look for work and rely on welfare payments for several years), or the inadequacy or ill effects of existing welfare policies.

Preschool through Grade 12 Education

The article focuses on descriptions of preschool, elementary, and secondary education programs (including public school programs, private school programs, charter schools, home schooling, voucher programs, year-round schooling, and other innovative education programs) and the merits of or problems with these programs.

- Articles focused on college education, community college, or postgraduate education (including medical school, law school, business school, or other graduate or professional programs) should NOT be coded as education.
- Articles about adult education programs should NOT be considered education.
- The "education policy" code is designed to loosely map on with Policy Agendas Topic Code 602: elementary and secondary education. Articles concentrating on federal legislation that pertains to preschool through grade 12 education should receive this code. Legislation that falls into this category includes bills that address the following topics: school funding disparities, education choice programs, high school dropout prevention, standards for public school teachers, federal spending on preschool through grade 12 education, student discipline, violence in schools, the Safe Schools Act, construction of public schools, high school scholarship programs, preschool programs, No Child Left Behind, Head Start, ways to measure student and teacher performance, college prep programs, charter schools, disparities in education (based on geography or demographic factors).
- To receive the "education problem" code, the main focus of the article should be related to problems in schools (preschool through grade 12) or the education system generally. This includes low student performance, violence and bullying in schools, crumbling school buildings, American children not performing as well as students in other countries, lack of funds for quality education, low teacher salaries, inadequate teacher training, high dropout rates, high truancy rates, students not being adequately prepared for college

or vocations by public schools, students not prepared to learn when they enter kindergarten or first grade, high rates of illiteracy, underperformance in science and math, lack of nutritious foods in school cafeterias, disparities in the quality of schools (based on geography and/or demographic factors), programs/courses being cut (such as music, foreign language, recess/phys-ed, etc.), older or inadequate textbooks.

Conflict Codes

Heated Conflict

This code is applied to conflict-focused descriptions of the interactions between political elites (meaning the article repeatedly—at least twice— uses words like "battle," "fight," "attack," "argument," or "enemies" to describe interactions between elites). Examples:

- "The perennial tension between governors and mayors exploded again last week in their responses to President Bush's proposal to turn over $15 billion of Federal programs to the states" (Pear 1991).
- "The whole question of work requirements for welfare recipients has generated intense conflict between Democrats and Republicans. House Democratic leaders attacked other parts of the Republican welfare bill, saying that those portions should have much more stringent requirements that people work as a condition of receiving cash assistance" (Pear 1995).
- "By proposing sharp slashes in Federal aid to education, President Reagan has run head on into the collective wrath of what former Representative Edith Green once called 'the educational-industrial complex'" (Hunter 1981).
- "Armed with conflicting economic studies, they waged verbal battle over job losses, inflationary effects and the question of whether Democrats or Republicans were the truer champions of workers at the lowest end of the scale" (Rasky 1989).
- "Still, Senator Daniel Patrick Moynihan, Democrat of New York, remains an angry opponent of the bill, which would abolish the longstanding Federal entitlement to assistance for any eligible poor family. 'I hope the President will veto this bill,' Mr. Moynihan told reporters. 'It's sure as hell cruel in the lives of American children'" (Toner 1995).

Generic Conflict Frame

This code refers to the overall theme and structure of the article. The headline and introductory paragraph(s) (first four sentences) are the keys to assigning this code. If either of these two elements of the article focuses on the struggle/tension/conflict/dispute between two or more actors or groups (such as congressional Republicans and congressional Democrats, the president and Congress, the Administration and the states, etc.), setting the article up as an examination of the "two sides of the issue," the article should receive this code. Examples:

- Lead: "The White House is clashing with governors of both parties over a plan to cut Medicaid payments to hospitals and nursing homes that care for millions of low-income people. The White House says the changes are needed to ensure the 'fiscal integrity' of Medicaid and to curb 'excessive payments' to health care providers. But the plan faces growing opposition. The National Governors Association said it 'would impose a huge financial burden on states,' already struggling with explosive growth in health costs" (Pear 2006).
- Lead: "As he completes his welfare plan, President Clinton must resolve a fight that has divided aides for months and has led one faction to accuse another of trying to rip holes in the social safety net. The fight is over whether families who follow all the rules can eventually be dropped from both welfare and a work program that Mr. Clinton is proposing" (DeParle 1994).
- Lead: "Even though President Clinton and Congress have agreed to spend $16 billion on health care for uninsured children in the next five years, a major dispute has broken out over whether the states or the Federal Government should decide how to use the money. Disagreements that have been bubbling just below the surface in the last two months will burst into public view this week, as the Senate Finance Committee votes on legislation to carry out the budget agreement" (Pear 1997).

Substantive Debate

This code is applied to debate over program efficacy and the potential effects of provisions. Here, the substance of a policy or a particular provision of a bill is described and elites discuss the potential merits and consequences of the bill's enactment. Substantive debate may also include controversy over the causes or severity of a societal problem, such as poverty, homelessness, lack of access to health care, etc. Examples:

- "The proposed new program, known as Part C of Medicare, was conceived by Representative Pete Stark of California, chairman of the Ways and Means Subcommittee on Health, who has long favored 'Medicare for all' as the best way to guarantee coverage for all Americans. 'Medicare is simple: no new rules, no new bureaucracy,' Mr. Stark said in an interview today. But many Republicans and some Democrats, including some in the Clinton Administration, say the Ways and Means Committee bill relies too heavily on the Government to cover the uninsured. They say it would be better to help people buy private insurance, rather than creating a new Federal health insurance program as part of Medicare" (Pear 1994).

- "House Republicans said today that they wanted to cut $16.5 billion from the food stamp program over the next five years by establishing strict new work requirements for recipients and by trimming the growth in benefits. The proposal represents a fundamental shift in the design of the program, which serves as the ultimate safety net for more than 27 million poor Americans. It is one piece of a huge bill intended to free poor people from dependence on Government while vastly increasing the power of state officials to run their own welfare programs free of Federal supervision. Democrats say the overall bill is cruel to women and children because it would, for example, scrap the national school lunch program and give the money to the states as well as bar the use of Federal money to provide cash assistance to unmarried teenagers" (Pear 1995).

Political Calculus

To receive this code, the article must contain a significant discussion (at least three sentences) of the political ramifications of a policy proposal or problem for a political actor (the president, congressional Democrats/Republicans, etc.). "Horserace" coverage (explaining which side is winning or losing) should receive this code, as should discussions of tactics designed to win popular support for a piece of legislation. Examples:

- "Their efforts to portray Mr. Bush as insensitive to the poor have generated little public reaction, and Mr. Bush appears to have suffered little political damage for his refusal to negotiate any alteration in his own plan. Fearful that they may now be perceived as the ones responsible for delaying a wage increase for the sake of a political battle over nickels and dimes, many Democrats are looking for a way out" (Rasky 1989).

- "The same political concerns that compelled President Bush to announce a "comprehensive health reform program" today also obliged him to be vague about many details. . . . While it has become politically necessary for candidates to address health care in general, it is virtually impossible for them to make specific proposals without offending somebody. Thus Dr. Louis W. Sullivan, the Secretary of Health and Human Services, and White House officials were unable to answer important questions today about how the President's plan would work" (Pear 1992).

- "For months the two chambers have played a game of legislative chicken, inviting each other to be the first to tackle this prickly issue in the midst of a Presidential election campaign. . . . Wary of forcing an election-year vote on an issue so sensitive to each of these powerful constituencies and unable to come up with a compromise, Congressional leaders all but gave up two weeks ago and pronounced a minimum wage increase dead for this year. Bush Raises Issue Again But then Vice President Bush shifted the political equation by endorsing an unspecified increase in the minimum wage, provided that it was accompanied by the 'training wage' for new workers set below the minimum standard" (Rasky 1988).

- "Mr. Bush's budget began an ideologically charged debate in a midterm election year, with his party's control of Congress at stake. . . . The Democratic Senatorial Campaign Committee quickly dispatched talking points tailored to hot Senate races. 'White House budget forces Santorum to choose between Pennsylvania and Bush,' said one set of talking points focused on Senator Rick Santorum of Pennsylvania, a Republican facing a difficult re-election fight" (Toner 2006).

Parliamentary Tactics

This code captures elements of congressional "sausage making" and strategizing by lawmakers and the administration. It should be applied to articles that are concentrated on the process of policy making within the legislative arena, particularly those that discuss the parliamentary tactics employed by the parties or the administration. This includes mentions of delay tactics, tactics used to limit debate, filibustering, methods of ensuring party loyalty, strategic timing of votes, strategic addition of amendments, party-line votes, disputes over committee jurisdiction, vetoes and veto threats, the imposition of deadlines on Congress, discussions of the administration lobbying Congress, etc. Articles that focus on deal making, logrolling, negotiations, and political alliances should receive this code. Examples:

- "President Bush has threatened to veto the House bill, developed entirely by Democrats, and a more modest bipartisan measure, expected to win Senate approval this week. Republicans tried to block consideration of the House bill and complained that it was being rammed through the House without any opportunity for amendment" (Pear 2007).
- Lead: "In a vote they acknowledged was largely symbolic, House Democrats today failed to override President Bush's veto of a bill raising the minimum wage. But the Democrats vowed to press for a compromise the President would sign. Moments after the 247-to-178 vote, 37 votes shy of the two-thirds needed to override the veto, Democrats in both the House and Senate made good on that pledge, by laying out plans for legislation aimed at persuading the President to bargain" (Rasky 1989).
- "Democrats were narrowly defeated today on another important amendment to the Republicans' welfare bill. Their amendment, rejected by a vote of 50 to 49, sought to prevent states from slashing their contributions to basic welfare programs. But the Republicans prevailed only after their leaders made new concessions on the issue to hold their party's moderates" (Toner 1995)

Spending, Deficit and Macroeconomic Codes

Spending and Deficit Estimates

This code is an indicator of whether the article provides factual information on the amount of new spending, size of spending cuts, or changes in the deficit that would result from the passage of a given policy. The article may also provide estimates of the amount of money that would be needed to correct a societal problem. To receive this code the article must provide a dollar estimate, such as a cost estimate, budget projection, or projected deficit figure that would result from new legislation. Specific estimates of the size of a cut to or expansion of a program can also receive this code (such as a percentage reduction/increase in the size of a program, figures detailing the size of a personnel cut/expansion, etc.). Examples:

- Size of cuts to a program: "Samuel R. Pierce Jr., Secretary of Housing and Urban Development, detailed the Administration's proposals at the beginning of today's hearing. He said that one effect of the proposals would be to reduce authorization for new public housing to 175,000 units, from the 260,000 units recommended by the Carter Administration; to raise rents for subsidized housing tenants to 30 percent of income, from 25 percent, and to make other cuts in Federal housing aid" (AP 1981).

- Size of cuts in spending: "David B. Swoap, Under Secretary at the Department of Health and Human Services, said at a briefing for reporters that the new restrictions in welfare eligibility would result in Federal savings of $1 billion by 1982, while states' costs will be reduced $850 million" (Weinraub 1981).

Tax Increases

Sub-code that identifies discussions of new taxes or proposed tax increases.

Tax Decreases

Sub-code that identifies discussions of proposed tax cuts or new tax credits.

Macroeconomics

Identifies references to anticipated changes in macroeconomic or business indicators (such as the unemployment rate, interest rates, or consumer sentiment) that could result or have resulted from a given policy.

Economic Focus

This code indicates that the spending, tax, or macroeconomic information provided is the focus of the article. To receive this code, such information must be contained in the headline or first four sentences of the article.

Substance Focus

The purpose of the article is to describe the substance of a piece of legislation. The focus is on providing information about the purpose of the legislation and the provisions contained within it. To receive this code, at least 50% of the article should focus on such substantive descriptions of the legislation. Substance-focused articles may also describe and discuss societal problems, such as poverty, homelessness, lack of access to medical care, etc. Such articles should give facts and figures about the reach or severity of the problem. "Human interest" stories that provide a portrait of the struggles faced by one family or one community—but do not provide information about the degree to which the example is indicative of a larger problem—should not receive the substance code. Examples:

- Policy substance: "The mammoth budget bills before the Senate and the House of Representatives this week follow the same themes, although they differ somewhat on the margins. These are the main elements: TAXES. Taxes would be reduced by $245 billion over sever years. Most families would get a tax cut of $500 a child. The tax rate on capital gains would be lowered, eligibility for individual retirement accounts would be expanded, the marriage tax penalty would be lessened and a tax credit would be allowed to offset some adoption expenses" (Rosenbaum 1995).

- Problem substance: "The poverty rate last year was three-tenths of a percentage point higher than in 1991, and it was the highest since the 15.2 percent level recorded in 1983. Many Parallel Data At the same time, the Census Bureau reported that the number of Americans without health insurance rose 2 million last year, to 37.4 million. . . . The new poverty data reflect trends already evident in other statistics. Unemployment last year averaged 7.4 percent, up from 6.7 percent in 1991, the year the recession ended" (Pear 1993).

- Policy substance: "The House education committee posted the proposals on its Web site this week. Among the most important changes in the draft are those to the law's accountability system, in which states judge whether schools have made 'adequate yearly progress' and can avoid sanctions. The draft would allow states to look beyond annual test scores and says bluntly that broader criteria 'may increase the number of schools that make adequate yearly progress'" (Dillon 2007).

- Policy substance: "The legislation, geared to help low-income students, seeks to reward good schools and penalize failing ones by carefully tracking improvement among students. It calls for annual testing and higher standards. Under the tentative proposal, students in the fourth and eighth grades would be required to take the current standardized national test every other year to serve as a benchmark for progress. This test would be taken in addition to a battery of yearly tests designed by the states" (Alvarez 2001).

Human Interest

The human-interest code should be applied to articles that contain descriptions of the people or communities affected by a policy or societal problem. Such articles "put a human face" on the policy or "paint a portrait" of the problem through example.

Human Interest Lead

Articles that contain such a description in the first four sentences should receive the human-interest lead code. Examples:

- "Nothing conspicuous in Christopher and Jennifer Cundiff's appearance says they are poor: not the neat navy blue soccer shirt and blue jeans Christopher wears, or Jennifer's white Mary Janes with a white rose button on each strap. Nor do they act deprived. Blond Jennifer, 6, bounds out of the schoolhouse door, while Christopher, 9, runs to his mother yelling, 'I got me an orange juice today!' But their mother, Norma Cundiff, says she gets every stitch of their clothing from a charity closet where the school keeps other kids' castoffs. Although their father, Robert, works as a dishwasher, the Cundiffs receive welfare, too: two free school meals a day and $60 a month in food stamps. Home is a tiny, cluttered white house, with castoff tattered sneakers piled in a corner and possessions covering every table" (Kilborn 1996).
- "SHALIA WATTS, a government employee from Sacramento, received some upsetting news in June: the health maintenance organization to which she belongs, Health Net, will no longer be available through her employer next year. At the same time, she said, she found that the monthly premium for the Blue Shield H.M.O. she chose as a replacement would be $110, almost double what she pays now. Co-payments for her prescription-drug plan already rose this year, she said, from $5 to a scale ranging from $10 to $30. 'I'm starting to feel the financial pressure; it really adds up,' said Ms. Watts" (Kobliner 2002).

Experimental Treatments

Treatments for Student Sample

Heated Debate, Spending

Headline: Partisan Battle on Education Heats Up

A hotly contested Democratic bill designed to reform K through 12 education by providing vastly more resources for schools and teachers is pitting Democrats against Republicans.

The debate has deteriorated into a partisan brawl centered on what the plan will cost and how it will be paid for. While Democrats argue the plan will reduce the federal deficit, Republicans vehemently reject these claims, saying the plan will cost far more than Democrats estimate.

Senate Democrats rely on the Congressional Budget Office projections, which show the costs more than offset by new taxes and fees and reduced government spending over the next ten years. "Republicans need to stop scaring everyone with their false claims about deficit spending," said Democratic Senator Mike Luna. "The CBO estimates show that our plan is fiscally sound and responsible."

Senate Republicans take a different view, saying that it is unlikely that Congress would follow through on many of the cost-saving measures included in the bill and that the projections are therefore misleading. "The Democrats are playing a shell game to hide the true cost of the legislation," said the chairman of the Senate Republican Conference. "We need firm commitments to rein in wasteful government spending as a precondition of increasing education funding."

Despite the controversy, the bill is expected to make it out of committee and to be considered by the full Senate in the coming weeks. Senate Democrats will have to close ranks and vote as a bloc to pass the bill without Republican support.

Civil Debate, Spending

Headline: Panel's Progress on Education Reflects Bipartisan Support

A bipartisan bill designed to reform K through 12 education by providing vastly more resources for schools and teachers is gaining momentum in the Senate.

Efforts to reform the education system have moved ahead rapidly, with committee members on both sides of the aisle making concessions designed to build a consensus on the main ingredients of legislation. Now members of the Senate are turning to the last key issue of the debate—how to pay for the plan—hoping they can reach a compromise there too.

Senate Democrats rely on the Congressional Budget Office projections, which show the costs more than offset by new taxes and fees and reduced government spending over the next ten years. "The CBO estimates show that the plan is fiscally sound and responsible," said Senate Democrat Mike Luna. "The Democrats are ready to move forward with it."

But Senate Republicans say that it is unlikely that Congress would follow through on many of the cost-saving measures included in the bill and that the projections are therefore overly optimistic. "We need firm commitments to rein in wasteful government spending as a precondition of increasing education funding," said the chairman of the Senate Republican Conference. "We can not take a wait-and-see approach to financing this program."

Leaders of both parties have pledged to find common ground and resolve their differences over spending before the upcoming Congressional break. "We are all working toward a common goal here," said Luna. "We won't let politics get in the way of that."

Heated Debate, Efficacy

Headline: Partisan Battle on Education Heats Up

A hotly contested Democratic bill designed to reform K through 12 education by providing vastly more resources for schools and teachers is pitting Democrats against Republicans.

The debate has deteriorated into a partisan brawl centered on whether several key provisions of the legislations will be effective. While Democrats argue the plan will help failing schools improve, Republicans vehemently reject these claims, saying the plan will lead to unintended, negative consequences.

"If we do nothing, I can almost guarantee you that test scores will continue to fall over the next 10 years, because that's what they did over the last 10 years," said Democratic Senator Mike Luna. "This plan will reverse that trend by providing our schools with the resources—like skilled teachers, new computers, and high speed internet access—that they need to provide all of our children with a first-rate education. Republicans need to stop their obstructionist tactics and get on board."

Republicans concede the need for education reform, but contend the plan could do more harm than good. "The overhaul is a risky experiment that Democrats are trying to ram through Congress," said the chairman of the Senate Republican Conference. "Many of the bill's provisions are untested, irresponsible, and could cause some students to fall further behind. We want to see more proven methods added to the legislation."

Despite the controversy, the bill is expected to make it out of committee and to be considered by the full Senate in the coming weeks. Senate Democrats will have to close ranks and vote as a bloc to pass the bill without Republican support.

Civil Debate, Efficacy

Headline: Panel's Progress on Education Reflects Bipartisan Support
A bipartisan bill designed to reform K through 12 education by providing vastly more resources for schools and teachers is gaining momentum in the Senate.

Efforts to reform the education system have moved ahead rapidly, with committee members on both sides of the aisle making concessions designed to build a consensus on the legislation. Now members of the Senate are turning to the last key issue of the debate—whether more can be done to insure the program's effectiveness—hoping they can reach a compromise there too.

"If we do nothing, test scores will continue to fall over the next 10 years, because that's what they did over the last 10 years," said Democratic Senator Mike Luna. "The Democrats feel confident that this plan will reverse that trend by providing our schools with the resources—like skilled teachers, new computers, and high speed internet access—that they need to provide all of our children with a first-rate education."

"I agree that we need to fix the educational system," said the chairman of the Senate Republican Conference, "but I don't want to rush into anything that hasn't been fully vetted. There's always a risk of unintended, negative consequences with a new program, which could cause some students to fall further behind. We want to see more proven methods added to the legislation."

Leaders of both parties have pledged to find common ground and resolve their differences before the upcoming Congressional break. "We are all working toward a common goal here," said Luna. "We won't let politics get in the way of that."

Heated Debate, Tactics

Headline: Panel's Battles on Education Highlight a Broader Split

A hotly contested Democratic bill designed to reform K through 12 education by providing vastly more resources for schools and teachers is pitting Democrats against Republicans.

The debate has deteriorated into a partisan brawl, with both sides employing parliamentary maneuvers designed to stall the other's efforts. Most recently, Senate Democrats swatted down Republican attempts to make fundamental changes to their legislation on Wednesday as the Finance Committee voted on a wide range of amendments that highlighted the deep partisan divide over the issue.

Democratic Senators characterized the amendments as "delay tactics." Senator Mike Luna said, "There is a substantial slow-walk taking place in this committee." The Committee Chairman said he hoped the committee would approve the bill this week, so it could be merged with a separate bill approved in July by the Senate Education Committee.

Republicans argue that Democrats are attempting to ram the legislation through the Senate. The chairman of the Senate Republican Conference, said: "Democrats have insisted on using education reform as a weapon against Republicans. They've been cynically exploiting people's fears, making responsible debate almost impossible."

Despite the controversy, the bill is expected to make it out of committee and to be considered by the full Senate in the coming weeks. Senate Democrats will have to close ranks and vote as a bloc to prevent a Republican filibuster from effectively killing the bill.

Civil Debate, Tactics

Headline: Panel's Progress on Education Reflects Bipartisan Support

A bipartisan bill designed to reform K through 12 education by providing vastly more resources for schools and teachers is gaining momentum in the Senate.

Efforts to reform the education system have moved ahead rapidly, with committee members on both sides of the aisle making concessions designed to build a consensus on the legislation. Now, Senate Democrats are working with Republicans to add a final series of amendments to the bill. The amendments are a compromise between the parties, designed to insure bipartisan support.

Democratic Senators expect the bill to move smoothly through the committee process. Senator Mike Luna said, "The committee is making excellent progress with regard to this bill." The Committee Chairman added that he believes the bill will be approved this week and will then be merged with a separate bill approved in July by the Senate Education Committee.

Republicans are also pleased with the progress of the bill. "We are all working toward a common goal here," the chairman of the Senate Republican Conference said. "Members of both parties are working together to guarantee that the legislation will enjoy broad support and will be considered in a timely fashion."

Thanks to the efforts of senators on both sides of the aisle, the bill is expected to make it out of committee and to be considered by the full Senate in the coming weeks. The measure is expected to pass easily with majorities of both parties approving the legislation.

Treatments for CCES

Panel's Progress on Education Reflects Bipartisan Support

WASHINGTON — A bipartisan bill designed to reform K through 12 education by providing more resources for schools and teachers is gaining momentum in the Senate.

Efforts to reform the education system are moving ahead rapidly, with committee members on both sides of the aisle making concessions designed to build a consensus on the legislation. Now members of the Senate are turning to the last key issues of the debate – how much it will cost and how to pay for it – hoping they can reach compromises there too.

Democrats rely on Congressional Budget Office projections, which show the costs more than offset by new taxes and reduced government spending over the next ten years. "The CBO estimates show that our plan is fiscally sound and that it will reduce the deficit in the long run," said Democratic Senator Thompson. "The Democrats are ready to move forward with it."

Republicans take a different view, saying it is unlikely that Congress will follow through on many of the cost-saving measures included in the bill and that the CBO projections are, therefore, misleading. "We need an objective measure showing the true cost of this legislation," said the chairman of the Senate Republican Conference. "And we need firm commitments to rein in wasteful government spending as a precondition of increasing education funding."

Leaders of both parties have pledged to find common ground and resolve their differences before the upcoming Congressional break.

FIG. C.I. Civil Debate, Spending.

Partisan Battle on Education Heats Up

WASHINGTON — A hotly contested bill designed to reform K through 12 education by providing more resources for schools and teachers is pitting Democrats against Republicans.

The debate has deteriorated into a partisan brawl centered on what the plan will cost and how it will be paid for. While Democrats argue the plan will reduce the federal deficit, Republicans vehemently reject these claims, saying the plan will cost far more than the Democrats estimate.

Democrats rely on Congressional Budget Office projections, which show the costs more than offset by new taxes and reduced government spending over the next ten years. "The CBO estimates show that our plan is fiscally sound and that it will reduce the deficit in the long run," said Democratic Stewart Thompson. "The Democrats are ready to move forward with it."

Republicans take a different view, saying it is unlikely that Congress will follow through on many of the cost-saving measures included in the bill and that the CBO projections are, therefore, misleading. "We need an objective measure showing the true cost of this legislation" said the chairman of the Senate Republican Conference. "And we need firm commitments to rein in wasteful government spending as a precondition of increasing education funding."

Despite the controversy, the bill is expected to make it out of committee and to be considered by the full Senate in the coming weeks.

FIG. C.2. Heated Debate, Spending.

Panel's Progress on Education Reflects Bipartisan Support

WASHINGTON — A bipartisan bill designed to reform K through 12 education by providing more resources for schools and teachers is gaining momentum in the Senate.

Efforts to reform the education system are moving ahead rapidly, with committee members on both sides of the aisle making concessions designed to build a consensus on the legislation. Now members of the Senate are turning to the last key issue of the debate – whether more can be done to insure the program's effectiveness – hoping they can reach a compromise there too.

"If we do nothing, I can almost guarantee you that test scores will continue to fall over the next 10 years, because that's what they did over the last 10 years," said Democratic Senator Thompson. "This plan will reverse that trend by providing our schools with the resources – like skilled teachers, new computers and high speed internet access – that they need to provide all of our children with a first-rate education."

Republicans concede the need for education reform, but contend the plan could do more harm than good if changes aren't made. "Some of these provisions could cause kids to fall farther behind by diverting funds from proven initiatives – like voucher programs – to risky, untested ones," said the chairman of the Senate Republican Conference. "We want to see more proven methods incorporated into the bill."

Leaders of both parties have pledged to find common ground and resolve their differences before the upcoming Congressional break.

FIG. C.3. Civil Debate, Efficacy.

Partisan Battle on Education Heats Up

WASHINGTON — A hotly contested bill designed to reform K through 12 education by providing more resources for schools and teachers is pitting Democrats against Republicans.

The debate has deteriorated into a partisan brawl centered on whether several key provisions of the legislation will be effective. While Democrats argue the plan will help failing schools improve, Republicans vehemently reject these claims, saying they will lead to unintended, negative consequences.

"If we do nothing, I can almost guarantee you that test scores will continue to fall over the next 10 years, because that's what they did over the last 10 years," said Democratic Senator Thompson. "This plan will reverse that trend by providing our schools with the resources – like skilled teachers, new computers and high speed internet access – that they need to provide all of our children with a first-rate education."

Republicans concede the need for education reform, but contend the plan could do more harm than good if changes aren't made. "Some of these provisions could cause kids to fall farther behind by diverting funds from proven initiatives – like voucher programs – to risky, untested ones," said the chairman of the Senate Republican Conference. "We won't let the Democrats ram this legislation through without a thoughtful debate."

Despite the controversy, the bill is expected to make it out of committee and to be considered by the full Senate in the coming weeks.

FIG. C.4. Heated Debate, Efficacy.

APPENDIX D

Alternative Model Specification (Estimating Support for the FMA)

TABLE D.1. **HLM Estimating Likelihood of Support for the FMA (Alternative to Model A).**

Variable	Coefficient
Ballot Measure State Dummy	0.08
	(0.16)
Year	−0.29*
	(0.13)
Ballot Measure State X Year	−0.39*
	(0.24)
Supports Civil Unions	−1.07*
	(0.15)
Opposes Marriage	2.44*
	(0.14)
Liberal	−0.29*
	(0.15)
Conservative	0.62*
	(0.12)
Constant	−1.79*
	(0.13)
Random Intercept	−14.9
	(26.5)
AIC	2241.2
N	2098

* Indicates statistical significance at the level of 90% confidence.

Detailed Predicted Probability Plots (Opposition to Health Care Reform)

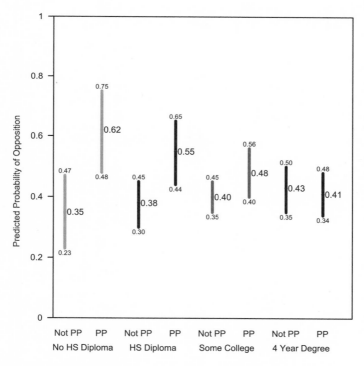

FIG. E.I. Predicted Probability of Opposition to Clinton Plan (detailed version).

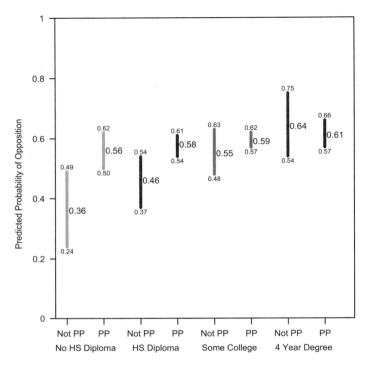

FIG. E.2. Predicted Probability of Opposition to the Affordable Care Act (detailed version).

Notes

Chapter One

1. Other generic frames include the economic frame, the human impact frame, the powerlessness frame, and the moral values frame (Neuman et al. 1992; Semetko and Valkenburg 2000).

2. In fact, Morris and Clawson (2005) analyze nine years of Congressional coverage from the *New York Times* and CBS Evening News during the 1990s. They find that "the democratic process is most often framed as conflict between parties and Congress and the president" (Morris and Clawson 2005, 297).

3. But note that in the context of campaign ads, negativity has also been found to have some positive effects, such as increased political knowledge (Lau et al. 2007) and increased political engagement (Brooks and Greer 2007).

4. But note that some scholars find just the opposite. See, for example, Druckman and Nelson (2003) and Nelson, Clawson, and Oxley (1997).

5. This focus on individuals calls to mind Iyengar's (1992) description of "episodic frames." I discuss episodic and thematic frames further in chapter 2.

Chapter Two

1. This is not to say that all policies (or even most policies) are solutions that are perfectly tailored to the problem at hand. On the contrary, policy problems and solutions are often uncoupled within the government arena as well (Cohen, March and Olsen 1972; Kingdon 1984).

2. This framing stands in contrast to "thematic frames," which focus on the broader societal factors, trends, and implications of events (Iyengar 1992).

3. A team of research assistants conducted the initial round of coding (the assignment of the "policy" and "problem" codes). The author conducted the second round of coding. This process is fully described in Appendix B.

4. A complete codebook with decision rules for assigning the codes described here is provided in Appendix B.

5. I did, however, look for instances of these codes in the problem-focused dataset and recorded the few instances of their occurrence.

6. As expected, this type of coverage was almost entirely absent from the problem-focused articles.

Chapter Three

1. UNC-Chapel Hill IRB number 11–1741.

2. The full text of the treatments is provided in Appendix C.

3. Note that party identification and ideology are not interchangeable, making the party cue distinct from the ideological cue. Roughly one third of the sample self-identified as independents. These individuals range from very liberal to very conservative. Further, most respondents (53%) placed themselves between 3 and 5 on the seven-point ideological scale, thereby placing themselves outside the "strong liberal" and "strong conservative" categories reported in table 9.

4. Note that the level of correlation between the conflict variable and the ideology variable is just 0.007, so the inclusion of both variables does not raise concerns about collinearity.

5. Respondents were asked whether they supported or opposed the legislation, therefore, a moderate response option was not provided.

6. These findings differ somewhat from those of the student sample. There, exposure to conflict had the strongest effect on liberals. Here, conservatives are more susceptible to the influence of the conflict frame. These differences might stem from demographic differences in the two samples or from the timing of the two surveys.

Chapter Four

1. These states are Arkansas, Georgia, Kentucky, Louisiana, Michigan, Missouri, Montana, North Dakota, Ohio, Oklahoma, Oregon, and Utah.

2. The amount of money spent on the 2004 referendum campaigns was quite modest as compared with more recent referendum campaigns. For instance, in 2008, campaign committees spent over $101 million in just four states considering bans related to gay partnerships (Quist 2009). The modest amount of money spent during the 2004 campaign cycle creates a hard test of the hypothesis I outline. Had committees spent larger sums of money on their initiative campaigns in 2004, the association of conflict with the issue would likely have been intensified.

3. Clearly, the sample used here is one of convenience. The searches de-

pended upon the availability of archives in Lexis Nexis and the analysis does not take account of exogenous differences between newspapers or media markets that could affect the number of articles on gay marriage (such as differences in the average number of pages in each newspaper). The exercise should be viewed as an informal test (not a comprehensive content analysis) designed to assure the reader that residents of ballot measure states were exposed to greater debate vis-à-vis residents of other states.

4. The conflict keywords used for the Lexis Nexis searches were: BODY (gay marriage OR "same sex marriage") AND (partisan OR battle OR argu! OR fight OR conflict OR controvers! OR heated OR feud OR fissure OR intractable OR outrage OR showdown OR standoff OR bitter OR fear OR anger! OR hate! OR assault! OR rage OR raging OR contentious OR condemn OR vehement! OR war).

5. Most of the state amendments contained the phrase "Only a marriage between one man and one woman shall be valid or recognized as a marriage," while the FMA states "Marriage in the United States shall consist only of the union of a man and a woman" (H. J. Res. 56 [108th]). State constitutions were accessed through the National Conference of State Legislatures website.

6. The 2004 poll randomly assigned half of the respondents a slightly different question wording, which did not influence responses. The alternative question wording is, "Do you think it should be LEGAL or ILLEGAL for homosexual couples to get married?" Also note that an analysis of various survey questions on the subject of the FMA conducted by The Pew Research Center found that respondents are less likely to favor the FMA when given the option of leaving the matter to the states (Pew Research Center 2004). Levels of support for the FMA reported here might, therefore, be lower than those reported in studies that rely on different question wordings. The question wording used does not impede my ability to test the hypotheses developed as the same question wording was used to assess support for the FMA in 2004 and 2005.

7. Missouri decided the matter with a popular vote held on August 3rd, 2004, and Louisiana put their measure to a popular vote on September 18, 2004.

8. I was sensitive to the possibility that respondents who oppose the FMA are not given a response option that clearly articulates their position on the issue. This could result in high levels of "don't know" responses among marriage supporters (see Berinsky 2004); however, table 4.2 shows there is not a significantly different percentage of "don't know" responses among marriage supporters and opponents.

9. I have replicated these findings with an HLM model, provided in Appendix D.

10. But note that prior to the amendment process, gay marriage was already prohibited by statutory law in all of the high-conflict states except for Massachusetts.

11. Note that the polls examined here sampled U.S. adults, not likely voters. The voters who endorsed the marriage amendments could have held different opinions on gay marriage than did the general public.

12. Readers might wonder why the state amendments succeeded if many citizens were turned off by the debates surrounding them. The simple answer is that individuals who strongly favored the marriage bans were mobilized by their presence on the ballot (just as conservative politicians hoped they would be). Marriage opponents, therefore, turned out in large numbers to vote for the measures, helping to ensure their success. Individuals with weaker, more moderate preferences—who are more susceptible to the influence of the conflict frame—were not mobilized by the debate. These individuals were probably less likely to turn out on Election Day, but are represented in the national survey data analyzed here.

13. Due to the smaller sample size that results from sub-setting the data, the standard errors reported in these models are bootstrapped in addition to being clustered by state.

14. The predicted probabilities plotted for civil union proponents are from Model D.

Chapter Five

1. This is not to say that members of the public viewed the president's proposal as a moderate reform. As discussed below, the Republican Party successfully perpetuated the idea that the plan was another "big government" liberal policy.

2. See Appendix E for a more detailed figure that includes confidence intervals around the predicted probabilities.

3. The survey asks respondents about a total of twelve substantive provisions. In preliminary models, I included measures of support for each of these provisions. For the sake of parsimony, the provisions that were not statistically significant predictors of opposition in the preliminary models are not included in the final model. However, the main findings reported here are not altered by the inclusion or exclusion of the full battery of substantive provisions.

4. See Appendix E for confidence intervals.

Chapter Six

1. This is the only national poll available through the Roper iPoll database with questions about the 1990 ADA.

2. The "second sweep" laws were identified using a retrospective rather than

contemporaneous measure of importance. Such laws were unlikely to receive news coverage at the time of passage.

3. The lists of important enactments for each Congress and the final passage vote totals are provided by David Mayhew on his personal website: http://davidmayhew.commons.yale.edu/datasets-divided-we-govern/.

4. Laws that passed by a voice vote were not included because the precise number of votes for and against the bill is not available in these instances.

5. I have restricted my analysis to comparisons of identical survey questions in the case of campaign finance reform because there are so few polls available on this topic. The use of identical questions should alleviate concerns that changes in levels of support over time might reflect changes in question wording. In all other cases, I have been careful to include only similarly worded questions and have omitted cases where the question wording changes systematically over time. Finally, note that in the case of the Bush tax cuts, the questions used to construct the time series come from polls of registered likely voters. All four polls were conducted by Greenberg Quinian Rosner Research. These are not the same polls reported in fig. 6.6.

Appendix A

1. The health keywords are loosely based on Policy Agendas subtopic 301. The education series corresponds to subtopic 602 and the welfares keywords correspond to subtopic 1302.

2. For instance, the education keywords include "bill," meaning a piece of legislation. If the search returned articles about men named Bill, such articles would represent "false hits." Articles about education bills in Congress would be "true hits."

3. The articles that comprise the dataset were downloaded from Lexis Nexis by hand. An automated parsing program was then used to compile the articles into an Access database.

References

ABC News. 1994. "ABC News Poll, September 1994 (ICPSR 3854)."

ABC News/Washington Post. 1993. "Heath Care Plan/NAFTA." November 11–14, 1993.

———. 2004. "ABC News/Washington Post Monthly Poll (ICPSR 04035-vi)." March.

———. 2005. "ABC News/Washington Post Monthly Poll (ICPSR 04326-vi)." April.

———. 2009. "Politics at Year's End: Double Punch of Economy, Health Care Sends Obama to New Lows in Approval." December 13.

Aborn, Richard M. 1994. "The Battle over the Brady Bill and the Future of Gun Control Advocacy." *Fordham Urban Law Journal* 22 (2): 417–39.

Achen, Christopher H. 1975. "Mass Political Attitudes and the Survey Response." *American Political Science Review* 69: 1218–31.

Ajzen, I., and M. Fishbein. 1980. *Understanding Attitudes and Predicting Social Behavior.* Englewood Cliffs, NJ: Prentice-Hall.

Alesina, Alberto, and Howard Rosenthal. 1989. "Partisan Cycles in Congressional Elections and the Macroeconomy." *American Political Science Review* 83: 373–98.

Alvarez, Lizette. 2001a. "Senate Moves Closer to Floor Debate on Education Bill." *New York Times*, April 26.

———. 2001b. "Lawmakers Break Impasse on Education." *New York Times*, November 28.

Anderson, John R. 1983. *The Architecture of Cognition.* Cambridge, MA: Harvard University Press.

Ansolabehere, Stephen, and Shanto Iyengar. 1995. *Going Negative: How Campaign Advertising Shrinks and Polarizes the Electorate.* New York: Free Press.

Associated Press. 2002. "1 in 4 Teachers Is Not Trained in Field." *New York Times*, August 22.

"Attitudes toward the Public Schools Survey." 2001. Survey by Phi Delta Kappa. Conducted by Gallup Organization, May 23–June 6.

Ball, William Benty. 1989. Testimony presented before the Senate Subcommittee on the Handicapped on S. 933. In "Should the Senate Approve the 'Americans with Disabilities Act of 1989: Con.'" *Congressional Digest* 68 (12): 295–97.

Baumgartner, Frank R., Suzanna DeBoef, and Amber E. Boydstun. 2008. *The Decline of the Death Penalty and the Discovery of Innocence.* New York: Cambridge University Press.

Baumgartner, Frank R., and Bryan D. Jones. 1993. *Agendas and Instability in American Politics.* Chicago: University of Chicago Press.

Becker, Elizabeth. 2001. "Millions Eligible For Food Stamps Aren't Applying." *New York Times*, February 26.

Bennett, W. Lance. 1990. "Toward a Theory of Press-State Relations in the United States." *Journal of Communication* 40 (2): 103–27.

———. 1996. *News: The Politics of Illusion.* 3rd ed. White Plains, NY: Longman.

Berinsky, Adam J. 2004. *Silent Voices: Public Opinion and Political Participation in America.* Princeton, NJ: Princeton University Press.

Berinsky, Adam J., and Donald R. Kinder. 2006. "Making Sense of Issues through Media Frames: Understanding the Kosovo Crisis." *Journal of Politics* 68 (3): 640–56.

Berkowitz, Edward D. 1994. "A Historical Preface to the Americans with Disabilities Act." *Journal of Policy History* 6 (1): 96–119.

Blendon, Robert J., Mollyann Brodie, and John Benson. 1995. "What Happened to Americans' Support for the Clinton Health Plan?" *Health Affairs* 14 (2): 7–23.

Boudreau, Cheryl. 2009. "Closing the Gap: When Do Cues Eliminate Differences between Sophisticated and Unsophisticated Citizens?" *Journal of Politics* 71 (3): 964–76.

Branigin, William. 2010. "Obama Reflects on 'Shellacking' in Midterm Elections." *New York Times*, November 3.

Brooks, Deborah J., and John Greer. 2007. "Beyond Negativity: The Effects of Incivility on Voters." *American Journal of Political Science* 51 (1): 1–16.

Bush, George H. W. 1990. "Remarks of President George Bush at the Signing of the Americans with Disabilities Act." Public Papers of the President.

Campos, Carlos. 2004. "Barbs Fly over Gay Marriage; GOP blasts Democrat in 12th District Race." *Atlanta Journal Constitution.* October 2.

Cappell, Joseph N., and Kathleen Hall Jamieson. 1996. "News Frames, Political Cynicism, and Media Cynicism." *Annals of the American Academy of Political and Social Science* (July): 546–71.

Carmines, Edward G. and James A. Stimson. 1980. "The Two Faces of Issue Voting." *American Political Science Review* 74 (1): 78–91.

CBS News/New York Times Poll. 1993. "November National Poll." November 11–14.

Chira, Susan. 1993. "Student Poll Finds Many Use Guns." *New York Times*, July 20.

Chong, Dennis, and James N. Druckman. 2007a. "Framing Theory." *Annual Review of Political Science* 10: 103–26.

———. 2007b. "A Theory of Framing and Opinion Formation in Competitive Elite Environments." *Journal of Communication* 57: 99–118.

CNN. 2009. "CNN Opinion Research Poll." 2009. http://i2.cdn. turner.com/cnn/2009/images/12/21/rel19a.pdf. December 16–20.

Cohen, James D., James G. March, and Johan P. Olsen. 1972. "A Garbage Can Model of Organizational Choice." *Administrative Science Quarterly* 17 (1): 1–25.

Converse, Philip E. 1964. "The Nature of Belief Systems in Mass Publics." *In Ideology and Discontent*. ed. David Apter. New York: Free Press of Glencoe.

Cook, Timoth E. 1998. *Governing with the News*. Chicago: University of Chicago Press.

Delli Carpini, Michael X., and Scott Keeter. 1996. *What Americans Know about Politics and Why It Matters*. New Haven: Yale University Press.

Druckman, James. 2001. "The Implications of Framing Effects For Citizen Competence." *Political Behavior* 23: 225–56.

Druckman, James N., and Kjersten J. Nelson. 2003. "Framing and Deliberation: How Citizen's Conversations Limit Elite Influence." *American Journal of Political Science* 47 (4): 729–45.

Durr, Robert H., John B. Gilmour, and Christina Wolbrecht. 1997. "Explaining Congressional Approval." *American Journal of Political Science* 41 (1): 175–207.

Entman, Robert M. 1993. "Framing: Toward Clarification of a Fractured Paradigm." *Journal of Communication* 43 (4): 51–58.

Erikson, Robert S., Michael B. MacKuen, and James A. Stimson. 2002. *The Macro Polity*. New York: Cambridge University Press.

Fasman, Zachary. 1989. Testimony presented before the Senate Subcommittee on the Handicapped on S. 933. In "Should the Senate Approve the 'Americans with Disabilities Act of 1989: Con.'" *Congressional Digest* 68 (12): 299–301.

Firestone, David. 2003. "Congressional Memo; Fate of Tax Credits Rests with Houses Divided." *New York Times*, June 16.

Fischle, Mark. 2000. "Mass Response to the Lewinsky Scandal: Motivated Reasoning or Bayesian Updating?" *Political Psychology* 21 (1): 135–59.

Fishbein, Martin, and Ronda Hunter. 1964. "Summation versus Balance in Attitude Organization and Change." *Journal of Abnormal and Social Psychology* 69 (9): 505–10.

Forgette, Richard, and Jonathan S. Morris. 2006. "High-Conflict Television News and Public Opinion." *Political Research Quarterly* 59 (3): 447–59.

Gamson, W. A., and A. Modigliani. 1989. "Media Discourse and Public Opinion on Nuclear Power: A Constructionist Approach." *American Journal of Sociology* 95 (1):1–37.

Gibson, James L. 1987. "Homosexuals and the Ku Klux Klan: A Contextual Analysis of Political Tolerance." *Western Political Quarterly* 40 (3): 427–28.

Goleman, Daniel. 1989. "Measure Finds Growing Hardship for Youth." *New York Times*, October 19.

Goode, Erica. 2001. "School Bullying Is Common, Mostly by Boys, Study Finds." *New York Times*, April 25.

Graber, Doris, ed. 1984. *Media Power in Politics*. Washington, DC: CQ Press.

Gronke, Paul. 2000. *Settings, Campaigns, Institutions, and the Vote: A Unified Approach to House and Senate Elections*. Ann Arbor: University of Michigan Press.

Haider-Markel, Donald P., and Mark R. Joslyn. 2001. "Gun Policy, Opinion, Tragedy, and Blame Attribution: The Conditional Influence of Issue Frames." *Journal of Politics* 63 (2): 530–43.

Haider-Markel, Donald P., and Kenneth J. Meier. 1996. "The Politics of Gay and Lesbian Rights: Expanding the Scope of Conflict." *Journal of Politics* 58 (2): 332–49.

Hallin, Daniel C. 1984. "The Media, the War in Vietnam, and Political Support: A Critique of the Thesis of an Oppositional Media." *Journal of Politics* 46 (1): 1–24.

Hamilton, Lee. 2010. "Results and Process Both Matter." Center on Congress at Indiana University. http://congress.indiana.edu/results-and-process-both-matter.

Harkin, Tom. 2012 "Americans with Disabilities Deserve Choices." *ABILITY Magazine* (June/July): 10–11.

Harris Interactive/HealthDay Poll. 2009. "Majority Supports Health Care Reforms: Negotiating for Lower Drug Prices Most Favored Idea." February 11.

Herszenhorn, David. 2009. "Opposing Claims Cloud the Debate on Overhaul." *New York Times*, November 23.

———. 2010. "Fact Check—Searching for Some Light amid the Heat." *New York Times*, January 29.

Hibbings, John R., and Elizabeth Theiss-Morse. 2002. *Stealth Democracy: American's Beliefs about How Government Should Work*. New York: Cambridge University Press.

Holsti, Ole R. 2004. *Public Opinion and American Foreign Policy*. Ann Arbor: University Michigan Press.

Hulse, Carl. 2003. "Pass the Sour Grapes, Not Sweet Potatoes." *New York Times*, November 27.

Hunter. 1981. "Cuts in U.S. Aid to Education to Have Wide Impact." *New York Times*, April 3.

Imparato, Andrew J. 2009. "Commentary: Kennedy a Champion for Disability Rights," Special to CNN. http://www.cnn.com/2009/POLITICS/08/29/kennedy.disabilities/index.html?iref=24hours. August 29.

Iyengar, Shanto. 1991. *Is Anyone Responsible?* Chicago: University of Chicago Press.

Iyengar, Shanto, and Donald Kinder. 1987. *News That Matters*. Chicago: University of Chicago Press.

Iyengar, Shanto, Helmut Norpoth, and Kyu S. Hanh. 2004. "Consumer Demand for Election News: The Horserace Sells." *Journal of Politics* 66 (1): 157–75.

Jacobe, Dennis. 2008. "Economy Widely Viewed as Most Important Problem." Gallup. Released March 13.

Jacobs, Lawrence R., and Robert Y. Shapiro. 1994. "Questioning the Conventional Wisdom on Public Opinion toward Health Reform" *PS: Political Science and Politics* 27 (2): 208–14.

———. 2000. *Politicians Don't Pander: Political Manipulation and the Loss of Democratic Responsiveness*. Chicago: University of Chicago Press.

Jacobs, Lawrence R., and Suzanne Mettler. 2011. "Why Public Opinion Changes: The Implications for Health and Health Policy." *Journal of Health Politics, Policy and Law* 36 (6): 917–33.

Jacoby, William G. 2000. "Issue Framing and Public Opinion on Government Spending." *American Journal of Political Science* 44 (4):750–67.

Jamieson, Kathleen Hall. 1992. *Dirty Politics*. New York: Oxford University Press.

Kahn, Kim Fridkin, and Patrick J. Kenney. 1999. "Do Negative Campaigns Mobilize or Suppress Turnout? Clarifying the Relationship between Negativity and Participation." *American Political Science Review* 93 (4): 877–89.

———. 2004. *No Holds Barred: Negativity in US Senate Campaigns*. Upper Saddle River, NJ: Pearson Prentice Hall.

Kaiser Family Foundation. 2007. "Kaiser Health Tracking Poll: Election 2008–December 2007."

———. 2009. "Kaiser Health Tracking Poll: Public Opinion on Health Care Issues." September.

———. 2010a. "March Kaiser Health Tracking Poll: Health Care Reform/Health Insurance." March.

———. 2010b. "Kaiser Family Foundation Poll: February Kaiser Health Tracking Poll Health Care Reform." February.

Kanin, Zachary. 2012. "After Months of Partisan Bickering, Congress Has Finally Agreed to Put a Slinky on an Escalator and See if It Goes Forever." *New Yorker*. January 16.

Kellstedt, Paul M. 2000. "Media Framing and the Dynamics of Racial Policy Preferences." *American Journal of Political Science* 44 (2): 245–60.

———. 2003. *The Mass Media and the Dynamics of American Racial Attitudes.* New York: Cambridge University Press.

Kim, Sung-youn, Charles S. Taber, and Milton Lodge. 2010. "Computational Model of the Citizen as Motivated Reasoner: Modeling the Dynamics of the 2000 Presidential Election." *Political Behavior* 32: 1–28.

Kinder, Donald R., and Lynn M. Sanders.1990. "Mimicking Political Debate with Survey Questions: The Case of White Opinion on Affirmative Action for Blacks." *Social Cognition* 8: 73–103.

Kingdon, John. 1984. *Agendas, Alternatives and Public Policies.* Boston: Little, Brown.

Kobliner, Beth. 2002. "Personal Business: Health Plans Are Offering Fewer Choices and Higher Costs." *New York Times*, October 6.

Krosnick, Jon A., and Donald R. Kinder 1990. "Altering the Foundations of Support for the President through Priming." *American Political Science Review* 84 (2): 497–512.

Kuklinski, James H., and Norman L. Hurley. 1994. "On Hearing and Interpreting Political Messages: A Cautionary Tale of Citizen Cue-Taking." *Journal of Politics* 55 (3): 729–51.

Kuklinski, James H., and Paul J. Quirk. 2000. "Reconsidering the Rational Public: Cognition, Heuristics, and Mass Opinion." In *Elements of Reason*, ed. A. Lupia, M. McCubbins, and S. Popkin. New York: Cambridge University Press.

Kuklinski, James H., Paul J. Quirk, David W. Schweider, and Robert F. Rich. 1998. "'Just the Facts, Ma'am': Political Facts and Public Opinion." *Annals of the American Academy of Political and Social Science* 560 (1): 143–54.

Kuklinski, James H., and Lee Sigelman. 1992. "When Objectivity Is Not Objective: Network Television News Coverage of U.S. Senators and the 'Paradox of Objectivity.'" *Journal of Politics* 54 (3): 810–33.

Lama, George de, and Lea Donosky. 1985. "Reagan Kills Farm Bill: No 'Bailout' for Farmers Deep in Debt." *Chicago Tribune*, March 7.

Lau, Richard, Lee Sigelman, and Ivy Brown Rovner. 2007. "The Effects of Negative Political Campaigns: A Meta-Analytic Reassessment." *Journal of Politics* 69 (4): 1176–1209.

Lebo, Matthew, and Daniel Cassino. 2007. "The Aggregated Consequences of Motivated Reasoning and the Dynamics of Partisan Presidential Approval." *Political Psychology* 28 (6): 719–46.

Los Angeles Times. 1993. "Senate Passes Brady Gun Bill Measure Moves into Conference with the House." *Baltimore Sun*, November 21.

Los Angeles Times Poll. 2001. March 3–March 5.

Loveless, Tom. 2006. "The Peculiar Politics of No Child Left Behind." The Brown Center of Education Policy: Brookings Institution.

Malone, Linda A. 1986. "A Historical Essay on the Conservation Provisions of the 1985 Farm Bill: Sodbusting, Swampbusting and the Conservation Reserve." *Kansas Law Review* 34: 578–97.

Marriott, Michel. 1990. "Dropout Fight Is Retooled for Grade Schools." *New York Times*, November 14.

Mayerson, Arlene. 1992. "The History of the ADA: A Movement Perspective." Disability Rights Education and Defense Fund. http://dredf.org/news/publications/the-history-of-the-ada/.

Miller, Joanne M., and Jon A. Krosnick. 2000. "News Media Impact on the Ingredients of Presidential Evaluations: Politically Knowledgeable Citizens Are Guided by a Trusted Source." *American Journal of Political Science* 44: 295–309.

Mitchell, Alison. 2001. "After the Nicknames." *New York Times*, March 9.

Montpetit, Eric. 2016. *In Defense of Pluralism: Policy Disagreement and Its Media Coverage*. Cambridge: Cambridge University Press.

Mooney, Christopher Z. 2000. "The Decline of Federalism and the Rise of Morality Policy Conflict in the United States." *Publius* 30 (1): 171–88.

Mooney, Christopher Z., and Mei-Hsien Lee. 2000. "The Influence of Values on Consensus and Contentious Morality Policy: U.S. Death Penalty Reform, 1956-82." *Journal of Politics* 62 (1): 223–39.

Morris, Jonathan S., and Rosalee A. Clawson. 2005. "Media Coverage of Congress in the 1990s: Scandals, Personalities, and the Prevalence of Policy and Process." *Political Communication* 22: 297–313.

Mutz, Diana C., and Byron Reeves. 2005. "The New Video Malaise: Effects of Televised Incivility on Political Trust." *American Political Science Review* 99 (1): 1–15.

National Organization on Disability. 1991. "1991 NOD Survey of Public Attitudes Toward People with Disabilities." May 15–June 18. [USHARRIS.91DISB.RC04.]

Nelson, Thomas E., Rosalee A. Clawson, and Zoe M. Oxley. 1997a. "Media Framing of a Civil Liberties Conflict and Its Effect on Tolerance." *American Political Science Review* 91 (3): 567–83.

———. 1997b. "Toward a Psychology of Framing Effects." *Political Behavior* 19 (3): 221–46.

Nelson, Thomas E., and Donald R. Kinder. 1996. "Issue Frames and Group-Centrism in American Public Opinion." *Journal of Politics* 58 (4): 1055–78.

Neuman, W. Russell. 1991. *The Future of the Mass Audience*. New York: Cambridge University Press.

Neuman, W. Russell, Marion R. Just, and Ann N. Crigler. 1992. *Common Knowledge: News and the Construction of Political Meaning*. London: University of Chicago Press.

Newport, Frank. 2008. "Obama Has Edge on Key Election Issues: Better Positioned than McCain on Top Two Issues: Gas Prices and Economy." Gallup.

New York Times. 2001. "Science Texts Contain Errors, Study Finds." January 16.

O'Connell, Sue. 2006. "The Money behind the 2004 Marriage Amendments." The Institute on Money in State Politics. January 27.

Papers of the Presidents of the United States: George W. Bush. 2004. U.S. Government Publishing Office.

Patterson, Thomas E. 1993. *Out of Order.* New York: Knopf.

———. 2007. "Political Roles of the Journalist." In *The Politics of News: The News of Politics,* 2nd ed., ed. Doris Graber, Denis McQuail, and Pippa Norris. Washington: CQ Press.

Pear, Robert. 1991. "The Nation: Washington's Plan to Funnel City Aid through the States Enrages the Mayors." *New York Times,* February 10.

———. 1992. "Bush Is Vague on Health Plan's Details." *New York Times,* February 7.

———. 1995. "House Republicans Propose Using a Work Requirement to Help Cut Food Stamp Costs." *New York Times,* March 6.

———. 2000. "Clinton Raises Stakes in the Battle over a Bigger Medicare Pot." *New York Times,* November 1.

———. 2004. "Education Chief Calls Union 'Terrorist,' Then Recants." *New York Times,* February 24.

———. 2007. "House Passes Children's Health Plan 225–204." *New York Times,* August 2.

———. 2010. "Colorado Voters Crave Reform of Health Care and Congress." *New York Times,* January 11.

Pear, Robert, and Carl Hulse. 2007. "Congress Set for Veto Fight on Child Health Care." *New York Times,* September 25.

Pear, Robert, and Robin Toner. 2004. "Partisan Arguing and Fine Print Seen as Hindering Medicare Law." *New York Times,* October 11.

Pew Research Center's Journalism Project Staff. 2010. "Six Things to Know about Health Care Coverage: A Study of the Media and the Health Care Debate." Pew Research Center Project for Excellence in Journalism. Released June 21.

Pew Research Center for the People and the Press. 2004. "Reading the Polls on Gay Marriage and the Constitution." Pew Research Center Pollwatch. July 13.

———. 2006. "Most Want Middle Ground on Abortion: Pragmatic Americans Liberal and Conservative on Social Issues." The Pew Forum on Religion and Public Life August 3.

———. 2009a. "Support for Health Care Principles, Opposition to Package: Mixed Views of Economic Policies and Health Care Reform Persist." The Pew Forum on Religion and Public Life. October 8.

———. 2009b. "Many Fault Media Coverage of Health Care Debate: Partisan Divide over Coverage." August 6.

———. 2009c. "News Coverage and News Interest—Matches and Mismatches—Top Stories of 2009: Economy, Obama and Health Care." Released Tuesday, December 29.

———. 2009d. "Health Care Debate Seen as 'Rude and Disrespectful.'" September 16.

———. 2009e. "Obama's Ratings Slide across the Board." July 30.

———. 2010a. "Six Things to Know About Health Care Coverage: A Study of Media and the Health Care Debate." Project for Excellence in Journalism. June 21.

———. 2010b. "Many Still Critical of Press Handling of Health Care—Health Care Finale: Heavy Coverage, Huge Interest." Tuesday, March 23.

———. 2010c. "Congress in a Wordle: Dysfunctional, Corrupt, Selfish." March 22. http://pewresearch.org/pubs/1533/congress-in-a-word-cloud-dysfunctional-corrupt-selfish.

———. 2010d. "The People and Their Government: Distrust, Discontent, Anger and Partisan Rancor." April 18.

———. 2011. "Public Sees Budget Negotiations as 'Ridiculous', 'Disgusting', 'Stupid': Leaders' Images Tarnished." August 1.

Postman, Neil. 1986. *Amusing Ourselves to Death: Public Discourse in the Age of Show Business.* New York: Penguin.

Presidential Remarks. 2011. "Remarks by the President: State Dining Room." http://www.whitehouse.gov/the-press-office/2011/08/08/remarks-president. August 8.

Princeton Survey Research Associates Poll. 2001. February 8–February 9.

Quist, Peter. 2009. "The Money behind the 2008 Same-Sex Partnership Ballot Measures." The Institute on Money in State Politics. November 18.

Rasky, Susan. 1989. "The Minimum-Wage Fight Isn't Really About Pay." *New York Times,* May 7.

Reagan, Ronald. 1991. "Why I'm for the Brady Bill." *New York Times,* March 29.

Redlawsk, David P. 2002. "Hot Cognition or Cool Consideration: Testing the Effects of Motivated Reasoning on Political Decision Making." *Journal of Politics* 64 (4): 1021–44.

Remarks by the President in State of the Union Address. 2012. The White House. https://www.whitehouse.gov/the-press-office/2012/01/24/remarks-president-state-union-address. January 24.

Rosenstiel, Thomas. 1994. "Press Found Putting Stress on Politics of Health Reform." *Los Angeles Times,* March 26.

Schattschneider, E. E. 1960. *The Semisovereign People: A Realist's View of Democracy in America.* New York: Holt, Rinehart and Winston.

Schemo, Diana Jean. 2001. "Bush-Backed School Bill Advances in Senate." *New York Times,* March 9.

———. 2002. "States Get Federal Warning on School Standards." *New York Times*, October 24.

Schudson, Michael. 2002. "The News Media as Political Institutions." *Annual Review of Political Science* 5: 249–69.

Scotch, Richard. 2001. *From Good Will to Civil Rights: Transforming Federal Disability Policy.* 2nd ed. Philadelphia: Temple University Press.

Seelye, Katharine Q. 1995. "Proposed Prayer Amendment Splits the Right." *New York Times*, November 22.

Seltzer, Richard 1993. "AIDS, Homosexuality, Public Opinion, and Changing Correlates over Time." *Journal of Homosexuality* 26 (1): 85–97.

Semetko, H. A., and P. M. Valkenburg. 2000. "Framing European Politics: A Content Analysis of Press and Television News." *Journal of Communication* 50 (2): 93–109.

Shanahan, Martha. 2013. "5 Memorable Moments When Town Hall Meetings Turned to Rage." *NPR News.* http://www.npr.org/blogs/itsallpolitics/2013/08/07/209919206/5-memorable-moments-when-town-hall-meetings-turned-to-rage. August 7.

Shapiro, Joseph. 1994. "Disability Policy and the Media: A Stealth Civil Rights Movement Bypasses the Press and Defies Conventional Wisdom." *Policy Studies Journal* 22 (1): 123–32.

Shoemaker, Pamela, and Stephen D. Reese. 1996. *Mediating the Message: Theories of Influence on Mass Media Content.* 2nd ed. White Plains, NY: Longman.

Skocpol, Theda. 1995. "The Rise and Resounding Demise of the Clinton Plan." *Health Affairs* 14 (1): 66–85.

Skocpol, Theda, and Lawrence R. Jacobs. 2012. "Accomplished and Embattled: Understanding Obama's Presidency" *Political Science Quarterly* 127 (1): 1–24.

Stubbs, Megan. 2012. "Conservation Compliance and U.S. Farm Policy." Congressional Research Service Report.

Sullivan, John L., James Pierson, and George E. Marcus. 1982. *Political Tolerance and American Democracy.* Chicago: University of Chicago Press.

Sullivan, Will. 2004. "Gay Marriage Draws Big Guns." *St. Louis Post-Dispatch*, June 27.

Swann, Nikola G. 2011. "United States of America Long-Term Rating Lowered to 'AA+' On Political Risks and Rising Debt Burden; Outlook Negative." Standard & Poor's. August 5.

Taber, Charles, and Milton Lodge. 2006. "Motivated Skepticism in the Evaluation of Political Beliefs." *American Journal of Political Science* 50 (3): 755–69.

Times Mirror Center for the People and the Press Poll. 1993. "Times Mirror News Interest Index December 1993." December 2–5.

Times Mirror Center for the People and the Press. 1993. "As Public Puzzles Personal Impact of Health Care Reform—Cautious Support for Clinton Plan." Release Friday, October 1.

———. 1995. "Media Coverage of Health Care Reform: A Final Report." *Columbia Journalism Review*. Supplement to the March/April issue: 1–8.

Toner, Robin. 1994. "Making Sausage: The Art of Reprocessing the Democratic Process." *New York Times*, September 4.

———. 1995. "Congressional Roundup—Democrats Try to Maintain Welfare Spending but Lose." *New York Times*, September 13.

———. 2006. "In Budget, Bush Holds Fast to a Policy of Tax Cutting." *New York Times*, February 7.

Tuchman, Gaye. 1978. *Making News: A Study in the Construction of Reality.* New York: Free Press.

Tversky, Amos, and Daniel Kahneman. 1981. "The Framing of Decisions and the Psychology of Choice." *Science* 211 (4481): 453–58.

———. 1987. "Rational Choice and the Framing of Decisions." In *Rational Choice: The Contrast between Economics and Psychology*, ed. R. M. Hogarth and M. W. Reder, 67–94. Chicago: University Chicago Press.

Vreese, C. H. de. 2002. *Framing Europe: Television News and European Integration*. Amsterdam: Aksant Academic.

West, Darrell M. 2010. "Broken Politics." *Governance Studies* 33: 1–8.

West, Darrell M., Diane Heith, and Chris Goodwin. 1996. "Harry and Louise Go to Washington: Political Advertising and Health Care Reform." *Journal of Health Politics, Policy and Law* 21 (1): 35–68.

Wilgoren, Jodi. 2001. "Education Study Finds U.S. Falling Short." *New York Times*, June 13.

Zaller, John. 1992. *The Nature and Origins of Mass Opinion*. New York: Cambridge University Press.

———. 1999. "A Theory of Media Politics: How the Interests of Politicians, Journalists, and Citizens Shape the News." Typescript.

Zaller, John, and Stanley Feldman. 1992. "A Simple Theory of the Survey Response: Answering Questions versus Revealing Preferences." *American Journal of Political Science* 36 (3): 579–616.

Zelman, Walter A. 1994. "The Rationale behind the Clinton Health Care Reform Plan." *Health Affairs* 13 (1): 9–29.

Index